The Growth Report
Strategies for Sustained Growth and Inclusive Development

The Growth Report

Strategies for Sustained Growth
and Inclusive Development

COMMISSION ON GROWTH AND DEVELOPMENT

Members of the Commission on Growth and Development

Montek Singh Ahluwalia, Deputy Chairman, Planning Commission, Government of India, New Delhi

Edmar Bacha, Director, Casa Das Garças Institute for Economic Policy Studies, and Senior Adviser, Banco Itaú BBA, Brazil; former Senior Adviser to the Minister of Finance in the implementation of the "Plano Real," and former President of the National Development Bank (BNDES)

Dr. Boediono, Governor, Bank Indonesia; former Coordinating Minister for Economic Affairs, Professor of Economics, Gajah Mada University, Indonesia

Lord John Browne, Managing Director, Riverstone Europe LLP; former CEO of British Petroleum p.l.c., United Kingdom

Kemal Derviş, Administrator, the United Nations Development Programme; former Minister for Economic Affairs and the Treasury, Turkey

Alejandro Foxley, Minister of Foreign Affairs; former Minister of Finance, Chile

Goh Chok Tong, Senior Minister in Cabinet and Chairman, Monetary Authority of Singapore; former Prime Minister, Singapore

Han Duck-soo, Former Prime Minister, Former Deputy Prime Minister, and Former Minister of Finance and Economy, the Republic of Korea

Danuta Hübner, Commissioner for Regional Policy, European Commission; former United Nations Under-Secretary General and Executive Secretary of the UN Economic Commission for Europe; former roles in the Polish government: Polish Minister for European Affairs, Minister for European Integration and Deputy Minister for Foreign Affairs, Minister–Head of the Chancellery of the President of the Republic of Poland, Deputy Minister for Trade and Industry

Carin Jämtin, Former Minister for International Development Cooperation, Sweden

Pedro-Pablo Kuczynski, Former Prime Minister and former Minister of Economy and Finance, Peru

Danny Leipziger, Vice President for Poverty Reduction and Economic Management, the World Bank Group; Commission Vice Chair

Trevor Manuel, Minister of Finance, South Africa

Mahmoud Mohieldin, Minister of Investment, Arab Republic of Egypt

Ngozi N. Okonjo-Iweala, Managing Director, the World Bank Group; former Minister of Finance and Foreign Affairs, Nigeria

Robert Rubin, Chairman of the Executive Committee, Citigroup Inc.; Former Secretary of the Treasury, United States

Robert Solow, Nobel Laureate in Economics; Institute Professor Emeritus, Massachusetts Institute of Technology, United States

Michael Spence, Nobel Laureate in Economics; Professor Emeritus, Stanford University; Commission Chair, United States

Sir K. Dwight Venner, Governor, Eastern Caribbean Central Bank, St. Kitts and Nevis

Ernesto Zedillo, Former President of Mexico; Director, Yale Center for the Study of Globalization, United States

Zhou Xiaochuan, Governor, People's Bank of China

MONTEK SINGH AHLUWALIA

EDMAR BACHA

DR. BOEDIONO

LORD JOHN BROWNE

KEMAL DERVIŞ

ALEJANDRO FOXLEY

GOH CHOK TONG

HAN DUCK-SOO

DANUTA HÜBNER

CARIN JÄMTIN

PEDRO-PABLO KUCZYNSKI

DANNY LEIPZIGER

TREVOR MANUEL

MAHMOUD MOHIELDIN

NGOZI N. OKONJO-IWEALA

ROBERT RUBIN

ROBERT SOLOW

MICHAEL SPENCE

SIR K. DWIGHT VENNER

ERNESTO ZEDILLO

ZHOU XIAOCHUAN

© 2008 The International Bank for Reconstruction and Development / The World Bank
On behalf of the Commission on Growth and Development
1818 H Street NW
Washington, DC 20433
Telephone: 202-473-1000
Internet: www.worldbank.org
      www.growthcommission.org
E-mail: info@worldbank.org
      contactinfo@growthcommission.org

All rights reserved

1 2 3 4 5 11 10 09 08

This report is a product of the Commission on Growth and Development, which is sponsored by the following organizations:

Australian Agency for International Development (AusAID)
Dutch Ministry of Foreign Affairs
Swedish International Development Cooperation Agency (SIDA)
U.K. Department for International Development (DFID)
The William and Flora Hewlett Foundation
The World Bank Group

The findings, interpretations, and conclusions expressed herein do not necessarily reflect the views of the sponsoring organizations or the governments they represent.

The sponsoring organizations do not guarantee the accuracy of the data included in this work. The boundaries, colors, denominations, and other information shown on any map in this work do not imply any judgment on the part of the sponsoring organizations concerning the legal status of any territory or the endorsement or acceptance of such boundaries.

All queries on rights and licenses, including subsidiary rights, should be addressed to the Office of the Publisher, The World Bank, 1818 H Street NW, Washington, DC 20433, USA; fax: 202-522-2422; e-mail: pubrights@ worldbank.org.

ISBN: 978-0-8213-7491-7
eISBN: 978-0-8213-7492-4
DOI: 10.1596/978-0-8213-7491-7

Library of Congress Cataloging-in-Publication data has been requested.

Cover design: Naylor Design

Contents

Preface

This report brings together the views of a Commission of 19 leaders, mostly from developing countries, and 2 academics, Bob Solow and me. The leaders carry with them decades of accumulated experience in the challenging work of making policies that influence millions of people's lives: their job prospects, their health, their education, their access to basic amenities, such as water, public transportation, and light in their homes; the quality of their day-to-day lives; as well as the lives and opportunities enjoyed by their children.

They have wrestled with the complexity of all the basic ingredients of growth strategies: budget allocations, taxes, exchange rates, trade and industrial policies, regulations, privatizations, and monetary policies, to name just a few. Sometimes these choices seem remote from people's day-to-day lives. But they have a tremendous impact.

It has been an honor for me to serve with them and also a breathtaking, high-speed learning process. I hope we are successful in sharing their insights, and those of a dedicated development and policy community of academics and practitioners, through this report and prominently through the papers, workshops, and case studies that go along with it.

The number of people living in high-growth environments or in countries with OECD per capita income levels has increased in the past 30 years by a factor of four, from 1 billion to about 4 billion. Growth has accelerated in the global economy and in an even wider set of developing countries. There is, perhaps for the first time in history, a reasonable chance of transforming the quality of life and creative opportunities for the vast majority of humanity. This report is an attempt to increase the likelihood that the hope becomes a reality.

Formidable challenges exist, to be sure: climate change, global governance, rising interdependence, volatility, risk, and inclusiveness which entails making sure everyone experiences the benefits. But these should not exceed our capacity for ingenuity, creativity, and empathy.

Our approach has been to try to assimilate and digest the cumulative experience of growth and development as well as careful and thoughtful policy analysis in a wide spectrum of fields. We then seek to share this understanding with political leaders and policy makers in developing countries, including the next generation of leaders; with an international community of advisers; and with investors, policy makers, and leaders in advanced countries and international institutions who share the same goals.

We started our work two years ago, in April 2006. We focused on sustained growth, not because it is the final goal, but because sustained growth enables and is essential for things that people care about: poverty reduction, productive employment, education, health, and the opportunity to be creative. We also agreed that our work needed to be informed by knowledge at the frontier in all the areas the Commissioners thought relevant for economic growth and development.

This led us to hold 12 workshops on a wide array of policy areas, all related to growth and development. In the workshops, more than 300 distinguished academics wrote and presented papers and discussed the issues. I want to take this opportunity to express my deep appreciation to my academic colleagues who joined in with enthusiasm, insight, and generosity in committing their time. Commissioners participated in the workshops as their schedules permitted. We focused on what we know and also on what we do *not* know. The whole enterprise would not have been possible without this rigorous assessment of the state of the art in growth-oriented policies.

The discussions among Commissioners over six meetings in New York, Singapore, Suzhou, London, and Washington, DC, and the 12 workshops helped clarify a large number of theoretical and empirical issues. It didn't take long to learn that in a number of areas the experts did not agree among themselves; nor do the Commissioners agree in all areas. The Commission does not think it has to settle the outstanding issues, or arbitrate ongoing debates. That will be dealt with over time, as academic and policy research progresses. It does believe that understanding the incompleteness of our knowledge, as well as the benefits and risks of certain kinds of policies, constitutes a useful and important input to those who have to take decisions under conditions of uncertainty and incomplete information.

The work has been rendered possible by the engagement and commitment of a large number of individuals. I am particularly grateful to the

Commissioners who had no hesitation in spending long hours in discussions in Commission meetings, in the workshops, and in helping me understand the nature of the economic, political, and social challenges that developing countries face.

The Commission and I have relied on a working group—I should say a *hard*-working group: Pedro Carneiro, Homi Kharas, Danny Leipziger, Edwin Lim, Paul Romer, Bob Solow, and Roberto Zagha. Together we have tried to assimilate a vast amount of material; organize and review the work prepared for the workshops; and decide on principal themes for the report. Bob Solow is revered for the depth of his economic insight and for his modesty and generosity. It is impossible to overstate the impact he has had on the evolution of the thinking of the Commissioners, and on me in particular.

Our editor, Simon Cox, played a particularly important role. Seldom does one find an editor who so deeply and thoroughly understands the logic and structure of the argument, and then expresses it with simplicity, clarity, and vividness.

A dedicated group of staff at the World Bank—Maya Brahmam, Muriel Darlington, Heiko Hesse, Teng Jiang, Diana Manevskaya, and Dorota Nowak—has organized every aspect of the work of the Commission, the workshops, the outreach strategy, publication of the report, and numerous working papers and reports. I thank them for their dedication, efficiency, and grace under intense pressure. Their efforts have produced the workshops, publications, communication and outreach activities, and the Web site, with more to come. In addition, the publication team has worked under enormous pressure and moving deadlines. I thank them for their patience, attention to detail, creativity in design, and can-do attitude. They are Aziz Gökdemir, Stephen McGroarty, Denise Bergeron, Nancy Lammers, and Santiago Pombo. I also want to thank Tim Cullen and his colleagues for their expertise and help in communicating the work of the Commission.

The whole enterprise was rendered possible by individuals and institutions that thought the project important, and decided to support it. I thank the governments of Australia, Sweden, the Netherlands, and the United Kingdom; the William and Flora Hewlett Foundation; and the World Bank Group for their interest and support.

It will be clear that it is not possible to name everyone who has contributed to this effort in the preface. I have included in an appendix the names of all those in various categories whose efforts made this possible.

I want to thank the vice chair of the Commission, Danny Leipziger. His many years of experience with growth and development, his generosity with his own time and in making available the considerable resources of the World Bank, have been invaluable. I should also say that this project, the Commission, owes its origin to Danny and his colleague Roberto Zagha in the Poverty Reduction and Economic Management network in the Bank. They thought and I agreed that the centrality of growth in achieving a number of development objectives, including poverty reduction, especially, and the availability of a growing body of research and experience, made this project timely.

Finally, I worked with one individual pretty much every day for two years. He is Roberto Zagha, the secretary to the Commission. Without even the slightest risk of exaggeration, none of this would have happened without him. The workshops, an essential ingredient of the process, were entirely his doing. His range of knowledge of the relevant work in development is amazing. His respect for, and his personal relationships with, leaders in academia and in practice have been the glue that held this all together. He is generous, modest, rigorous in his thinking and interactions, and cares deeply about the end goal. For me it has been enormously rewarding to be his working partner in this effort.

Michael Spence
June 2008

Abbreviations

AGOA	Africa Growth and Opportunity Act
AusAID	Australian Agency for International Development
CAGR	Compound annual growth rate
CO2	Carbon dioxide
Dev11	Algeria, Bangladesh, the Arab Republic of Egypt, Indonesia, the Islamic Republic of Iran, Malaysia, Pakistan, the Philippines, Romania, Thailand, and Turkey
DFID	U.K. Department for International Development
DPT	Diphtheria, pertussis (or whooping cough), and tetanus (vaccine)
EITI	Extractive Industries Transparency Initiative
EU	European Union
FDI	Foreign direct investment
GDP	Gross domestic product
GHGs	Greenhouse gases
Growth 13	Botswana; Brazil; China; Hong Kong, China; Indonesia; Japan; Korea, Rep. of; Malaysia; Malta; Oman; Singapore; Taiwan, China; and Thailand
HIV/AIDS	Human immunodeficiency virus/acquired immunodeficiency syndrome
IAER	Institute of Applied Economic Research (Brazil)
ICT	Information, communications, and technology
IMF	International Monetary Fund
IPCC	Intergovernmental Panel on Climate Change
MDG	Millennium Development Goal
MUV	Manufacturing unit value
NGO	Nongovernmental organization
OECD	Organisation for Economic Co-operation and Development
PPPs	Purchasing power parities
RCA	Revealed comparative advantage
SAR	Special Administrative Region
SIDA	Swedish International Development Cooperation Agency
SSA	Sub-Saharan Africa
UN	United Nations
UNDP	United Nations Development Programme
WTO	World Trade Organization
WWII	World War Two

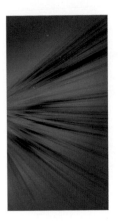

Overview

Since 1950, 13 economies have grown at an average rate of 7 percent a year or more for 25 years or longer. At that pace of expansion, an economy almost doubles in size every decade. This report is about sustained, high growth of this kind: its causes, consequences, and internal dynamics.[1] One might call it a report on "economic miracles," except that we believe the term is a misnomer. Unlike miracles, sustained, high growth can be explained and, we hope, repeated.

Growth is not an end in itself. But it makes it possible to achieve other important objectives of individuals and societies. It can spare people *en masse* from poverty and drudgery. Nothing else ever has. It also creates the resources to support health care, education, and the other Millennium Development Goals to which the world has committed itself. In short, we take the view that growth is a necessary, if not sufficient, condition for broader development, enlarging the scope for individuals to be productive and creative.

---

1 It reflects the views of a Commission consisting of 19 well-known and experienced policy, government, and business leaders, mostly from the developing world, and two renowned economists. It was written over two years during which the Commission interacted, consulted with, and learned from leading academics, business leaders, policy makers, and NGOs. The report reflects the learning over this period and is informed by the Commission members' own experience.

Growth Dynamics and the Global Economy

The report identifies some of the distinctive characteristics of high-growth economies and asks how other developing countries can emulate them. It does not provide a formula for policy makers to apply—no generic formula exists. Each country has specific characteristics and historical experiences that must be reflected in its growth strategy. But the report does offer a framework that should help policy makers create a growth strategy of their own. It will not give them a full set of answers, but it should at least help them ask the right questions. Fast, sustained growth does not happen spontaneously. It requires a long-term commitment by a country's political leaders, a commitment pursued with patience, perseverance, and pragmatism.

Growth of 7 percent a year, sustained over 25 years, was unheard of before the latter half of the 20th century. It is possible only because the world economy is now more open and integrated. This allows fast-growing economies to import ideas, technologies, and know-how from the rest of the world. One conduit for this knowledge is foreign direct investment, which several high-growth economies actively courted; another is foreign education, which often creates lasting international networks. Since learning something is easier than inventing it, fast learners can rapidly gain ground on the leading economies. Sustainable, high growth is catch-up growth. And the global economy is the essential resource.

The open world economy also offers developing countries a deep, elastic market for their exports. Since the division of labor is limited by the extent of the market, this extensive world demand allows countries to specialize in new export lines and improve their productivity in manifold ways.

Is a turn outward the only route to growth? Some economies have instead looked inward, competing with imports in the home market, rather than competing for foreign custom in the world market. These strategies have occasionally succeeded in spurring investment, increasing the size and efficiency of domestic producers. They also avoid the risks and dislocations of opening up to foreign competition too abruptly. Nevertheless, growth strategies that rely exclusively on domestic demand eventually reach their limits. The home market is usually too small to sustain growth for long, and it does not give an economy the same freedom to specialize in whatever it is best at producing.

Catch-up growth is also made possible by an abundant labor supply. As the economy expands and branches out, new ventures draw underemployed workers out of traditional agriculture into more productive work in the cities. Resources, especially labor, must be mobile. No country has industrialized without also urbanizing, however chaotically.

Economies in high-growth mode are transforming themselves structurally. To quote from the report, "The growth of GDP may be measured up in the macroeconomic treetops, but all the action is in the microeco-

"Our objective was not to summarize the state of knowledge, but to prepare a report short enough for prime ministers and presidents to read, a report which might help them think through the nature of growth strategies and ask the right questions of their ministers and advisers."

—Montek Singh Ahluwalia

nomic undergrowth, where new limbs sprout, and dead wood is cleared away." Most growth-oriented policies and reforms are designed to foster this microeconomics of creation and destruction, and, crucially, to protect people who are adversely affected by these dynamics.

Thanks to abundant labor and deep world demand, the speed of growth in the early stages of development is limited primarily by the pace of investment (public and private together). This investment is itself affected by the availability of savings. High-growth economies typically set aside a formidable share of their income: a national saving rate of 20–25 percent or higher, is not unusual. In principle, countries could rely more on foreign capital to finance their investment needs. But capital inflows over the past several decades have a mixed record. Our view is that foreign saving is an imperfect substitute for domestic saving, including public saving, to finance the investment a booming economy requires.

Leadership and Effective Government

Successful cases share a further characteristic: an increasingly capable, credible, and committed government. Growth at such a quick pace, over such a long period, requires strong political leadership. Policy makers have to choose a growth strategy, communicate their goals to the public, and convince people that the future rewards are worth the effort, thrift, and economic upheaval. They will succeed only if their promises are credible and inclusive, reassuring people that they or their children will enjoy their full share of the fruits of growth.

Such leadership requires patience, a long planning horizon, and an unwavering focus on the goal of inclusive growth. In several cases, fast-growing economies were overseen by a single-party government that could expect to remain in power for a long period of time. In other cases, multi-party democracies found ways to be patient and maintain a consistent focus over time. Rival political parties can, for example, agree on a bipartisan growth strategy, which they each follow during their term in power. Even if a formal pact is never made, a successful growth strategy, commanding the confidence of the public, may outlast the government that introduced it. Experience suggests that strong, technocratic teams, focused on long-term growth, can also provide some institutional memory and continuity of policy. This stability and experience can be particularly valuable during political upheavals, because new systems of collective decision making can take a long while to bed down and function efficiently.

Just as growth is not the ultimate objective, reforms aren't either. Both are means to ends. Reforms may be admirable and represent major achievements, but if growth does not accelerate, or if large numbers of people do not feel any improvement in their circumstances, then there is more work to do. Relying on markets to allocate resources efficiently is clearly necessary (there is no known, effective substitute), but that is not the same thing as letting some combination of markets and a menu of reforms determine outcomes.

Wedded to the goal of high growth, governments should be pragmatic in their pursuit of it. Orthodoxies apply only so far. This report is the product of two years of inquiry and debate, led by experienced policy makers, business people and two Nobel prize-winning academics, who heard from leading authorities on everything from macroeconomic policy to urbanization. If there were just one valid growth doctrine, we are confident we would have found it.

Economists know how markets work, and they can say with some confidence how a mature market economy will respond to their policy prescriptions. But mature markets rely on deep institutional underpinnings, institutions that define property rights, enforce contracts, convey prices, and bridge informational gaps between buyers and sellers.

Developing countries often lack these market and regulatory institutions. Indeed, an important part of development is precisely the creation of these institutionalized capabilities. Even without them, growth can occur, and these institutions can co-evolve with the economy as it expands. However, we do not know in detail how these institutions can be engineered, and policy makers cannot always know how a market will function without them. The impact of policy shifts and reforms is therefore harder to predict accurately in a developing economy. At this stage, our models or predictive devices are, in important respects, incomplete.

It is, therefore, prudent for governments to pursue an experimental approach to the implementation of economic policy. The principle is expressed well by Deng Xiaoping's oft-quoted dictum to "cross the river by feeling for the stones." Governments should sometimes proceed step by step, avoiding sudden shifts in policy where the potential risks outweigh the benefits. This will limit the potential damage of any policy misstep, making it easier for the government and the economy to right itself. Likewise, each footfall should represent a small trial or experiment, a "feeling about" for the best way forward.

Making policy is only part of the battle. Policies must also be faithfully implemented and tolerably administered. An effective government apparatus is not built overnight and requires constant attention. A culture of honest public service must be fostered and maintained. The administration must also attract and retain talented people, by offering better pay, promotions, and recognition to officials who can measurably improve the public sector's performance.

Government is not the proximate cause of growth. That role falls to the private sector, to investment and entrepreneurship responding to price signals and market forces. But stable, honest, and effective government is critical in the long run. The remit of the government, for example, includes maintaining price stability and fiscal responsibility, both of which influence the risks and returns faced by private investors.

In recent decades governments were advised to "stabilize, privatize and liberalize." There is merit in what lies behind this injunction—governments should not try to do too much, replacing markets or closing the economy off from the rest of the world. But we believe this prescription defines the role of government too narrowly. Just because governments are sometimes clumsy and sometimes errant, does not mean they should be written out of the script. On the contrary, as the economy grows and develops, active, pragmatic governments have crucial roles to play.

Sustained, high growth is not easy. If it were, the list of successful cases would be longer. Some countries struggle to start growth; others fail to sustain it. Some grow quickly, but reach a plateau when they reach middle-income. A fast-growing economy is a moving target. Bad policies are often good policies applied for too long. And just as a country's growth strategy must evolve with the economy, a country's politics must as well. Prosperity will create a middle class whose voice will need to be recognized in the political process, both locally and centrally.

Having described the art of policy making, we now turn to policy ingredients themselves. The number of desirable reforms and outlays a government might consider at any point of time will vastly exceed its reach and budget. A coherent growth strategy will therefore set priorities, deciding where to devote a government's energies and resources. These choices are extremely important. They should also be country- and context-specific, responding to widely varying initial conditions. This report cannot therefore set priorities for policy makers. It can only identify the policies that need attention.

The policy underpinnings of sustained, high growth create an environment for high levels of investment, job creation, competition, mobility of resources, social protections, equity, and inclusiveness. It would be going a little too far to describe them all as necessary conditions. Our view is that an understanding of the dynamics and a focused attention on the policy foundations will significantly increase the chances of accelerating growth. Conversely, persistent inattention to them will eventually harm it. There are many different recipes for pasta. The precise ingredients and timing are different for each. But if you leave out the salt or boil it too long, the results are distinctly inferior.

Selected Policy Ingredients

No country has sustained rapid growth without also keeping up impressive rates of public investment—in infrastructure, education, and health. Far from crowding out private investment, this spending crowds it *in*. It paves the way for new industries to emerge and raises the return to any private venture that benefits from healthy, educated workers, passable roads, and reliable electricity.

Unfortunately, we discovered, infrastructure spending is widely neglected. Often it is not even measured. We also found that the quantity of education (years of schooling, rates of enrollment) in many countries was more impressive than the results: literacy, numeracy, and other cognitive skills. Needless to say, it is the results that matter to growth.

Health is of deep value to people, regardless of its impact on growth. Nonetheless, the economic consequences of hunger, malnutrition, and disease should not be forgotten. We wish to highlight one example in particular: if children are undernourished in the womb or in infancy, their cognitive development can be permanently impaired. This reduces their productivity and their ability to benefit from an education. It is also deeply unfair. The rapid rise in world food prices, which has made it harder for poor families to feed themselves adequately, therefore poses a first-order threat to long-term growth. While higher food prices may create long-run opportunities for developing countries, the suddenness of the increase and the inevitable lags in raising supply have produced an emergency in the short term that needs to be addressed.

Growth entails a structural transformation of the economy, from agriculture to manufacturing, from a rural workforce to an urban one. This transformation is the result of competitive pressure. Governments committed to growth must therefore liberalize product markets, allowing new, more productive firms to enter and obsolete firms to exit. They must also create room to maneuver in the labor market, so that new industries can quickly create jobs and workers can move freely to fill them. These reforms are easier to recommend than to enact. If a wholesale overhaul of the labor laws is politically impossible, policy makers should instead seek a pragmatic compromise that fulfills the aspirations of jobseekers and is not vetoed by politically influential jobholders.

While creative destruction is economically natural, it doesn't feel natural to those displaced in the process. Policy makers should resist calls to protect industries, firms, or jobs, but they should endeavor to protect *people*. Perhaps the best protections a government can provide are education, which makes it easier to pick up new skills, and a strong rate of job creation, which makes it easy to find new employment. Beyond that, governments should also establish social safety nets—which provide a source of income to people between jobs—and ensure uninterrupted access to basic services. These policies are both ethical and practical. Without them, popular support for a growth strategy will quickly erode.

Economic insecurity is not confined to the developing world. In a number of high-income countries, inequality is rising as median wages stagnate.

The cause of these trends is disputed. But whatever the true culprit, the public tends to blame globalization. As a result, they are increasingly skeptical of the case for an open economy, despite the great gains it brings. The Commission thinks governments should try harder to spread the benefits of globalization more equitably and to protect people from economic dislocation, whatever the cause. Support for an open global economy depends upon it.

The Commission strongly believes that growth strategies cannot succeed without a commitment to equality of opportunity, giving everyone a fair chance to enjoy the fruits of growth. But equal opportunities are no guarantee of equal outcomes. Indeed, in the early stages of growth, there is a natural tendency for income gaps to widen. Governments should seek to contain this inequality, the Commission believes, at the bottom and top ends of the income spectrum. Otherwise, the economy's progress may be jeopardized by divisive politics, protest, and even violent conflict. Again, if the ethical case does not persuade, the pragmatic one should.

The education of girls provides one strong test of a government's commitment to equality of opportunity. Many formidable obstacles stop girls from completing their schooling: family financial pressure, lack of safety, even things as basic as inadequate toilet facilities. But if these obstacles can be overcome, the payoff is very high. Educated women have fewer, healthier children, and they have them at older ages. Their children are then more successful in school, largely because they benefit from their mother's education. Educating girls and integrating them into the labor force is thus one way to break an intergenerational cycle of poverty.

Governments in the high-growth economies were not free-market purists. They tried a variety of policies to help diversify exports or sustain competitiveness. These included industrial policies to promote investment in new sectors, and managed exchange rates, shepherded by selected capital controls and reserve accumulation. These policies are highly controversial. Within the Commission and the broader policy community, there is a wide range of opinion about their benefits and risks. We have tried to set out the rationale for these policies and to identify the potential problems they create. An awareness of both seems important and useful. If they try these expedients, governments should be clear about what they are trying to achieve and be quick to reverse course if the intended results do not materialize. The policies should also be transitory, unless there are compelling externalities or market failures that require their retention. Any profit-seeking activity that needs permanent subsidies or price distortions to survive does not deserve to do so.

The environment has often been neglected in the early stages of growth, leaving air thick with particulates and water contaminated with effluents. We believe this is a mistake, and one that is extremely expensive to fix in the future. The report argues that growth strategies should take account of the cost of pollution from the outset, even if they do not immediately adopt the toughest environmental standards upheld in rich countries. The report also calls on developing countries to wean themselves off fuel subsidies. These subsidies impose a mounting fiscal burden as energy prices rise, diverting money that would be better spent on neglected public infrastructure. They also skew patterns of private investment in the economy towards smoke-stack industries and energy-intensive techniques. Finally, these energy subsidies will inhibit the participation of developing countries in global efforts to cut greenhouse gases.

Countries Facing Special Challenges

The countries to whom this report is addressed all share a need for faster growth. But they are not otherwise alike. Some are large, others small; some rich in natural resources, others with nothing but their labor to sell. Some are keen to know how to start growth; others worried about how to recover it. The report identifies four groupings of countries that appear to face particular challenges in generating and sustaining high growth. These are:

1. *African Countries*: The countries of Sub-Saharan Africa must contend with unhelpful borders, bequeathed by colonialism, and the mixed blessing of unusually rich natural resources. A striking proportion of Africa's population lives in landlocked countries that under different historical circumstances would probably be provinces of a larger political unit. But Africa's immediate past is more hopeful. It has grown by 6 percent a year in recent years and its commodity exports are fetching high prices. We look at the steps required to sustain this momentum, focusing in particular on how African countries can raise investment and diversify their exports.

2. *Small States*: The world economy is dotted with a large number of very small states, where the per capita cost of government and public services is inevitably high. Because of their small size, they have little scope to diversify their economies, which leaves them highly vulnerable to economic shocks. The answers lie in embracing the world economy, forming regional clubs, and outsourcing some government functions.

3. *Countries rich in natural resources*: Economies blessed with abundant oil, minerals, or other natural resources should be able to invest the "rents" or proceeds at home, raising their growth potential. But the historical experience has most often been the reverse. The pitfalls are well known. Sometimes the state sells extraction rights too cheaply or taxes resource revenues too lightly. Sometimes the money it raises is stolen or squandered by rent-seeking elites and vested interests. When the

money is invested, it is not always invested wisely or transparently. And by providing a ready source of foreign-exchange, natural resources can also reduce incentives for diversifying exports, a predicament known as "Dutch disease." States will improve on this sorry historical record only if they capture an appropriate share of the resource rents; save a judicious amount overseas; and set clear, growth-oriented priorities for absorbing the remainder at home.

4. *Middle-income countries:* Economies often struggle to maintain their growth momentum as they narrow the gap with high-income countries. As wages rise, they steadily lose their comparative advantage in labor-intensive industries. Eventually those industries fade away. Increasingly, growth must spring from knowledge, innovation, and a deeper stock of physical and human capital. Services also assume a more prominent role in the economic mix. The growth strategies that served an economy well at lower income levels cease to apply. Instead of providing targeted support to labor-intensive sectors, governments must expand higher education to support the growing service sector of the economy. Skills must be upgraded across the spectrum of employment. Otherwise, the disappearance of unskilled manufacturing jobs will leave the less skilled and less educated part of the population stranded without good employment options.

New Global Challenges

Countries embarking on a high-growth strategy today must overcome some global trends their predecessors did not face. These include global warming; the falling relative price of manufactured goods and rising relative price of commodities, including energy; swelling discontent with globalization in advanced and some developing economies; the aging of the world's population, even as poorer countries struggle to cope with a "youth bulge"; and a growing mismatch between global problems—in economics, health, climate change, and other areas—and weakly coordinated international responses.

Global Warming and Climate Change

Climate change is the quintessential global challenge: the harm greenhouse gases do is not confined to the country that emitted them. Indeed, poorer countries, which have contributed least to the problem, may suffer the most. They may need to take defensive action against the consequences of climate change sooner rather than later. We don't know how soon. But international contingency plans—to provide help to a country in case of need—are underway and should be speeded up.

Preventing climate change (or "mitigation" as the experts call it) is better than palliating its effects. But how can we cut carbon emissions to safe levels by midcentury while also accommodating the growth of developing countries? At the moment the debate has reached a conceptual impasse.

Technology offers one answer. Advanced economies should promote the creation of new techniques for cutting carbon and saving energy. The world needs to reduce radically the energy- and carbon-intensity of global growth. That is the only way developing countries can grow rapidly without subjecting the world to potentially catastrophic global warming.

Second, global mitigation efforts need to satisfy the dual criteria of efficiency (that is, cutting the most emissions at the least cost) and fairness. In the interests of fairness, advanced economies, which are responsible for most of the problem, should take the lead in setting medium-term targets for cuts in their own emissions.

Many people also argue that developing countries should commit to longer term, 50-year emissions targets. After all, these countries are responsible for a growing share of gases in the atmosphere. But this, we feel, is the wrong approach. Poor developing countries can make a bigger, quicker contribution by cooperating in cross-border mitigation projects. These projects meet the dual criteria of efficiency and fairness. The cuts are made in poor countries, which is efficient. But the costs are borne by richer countries, which is fair. Beyond this contribution, developing countries also need to improve energy efficiency, import new technologies rapidly, and eliminate energy subsidies.

Convergence in long-term per capita emissions is both feasible and desirable. As countries approach high-income levels, they should be entitled to the same per capita emissions as other advanced economies. These entitlements must be consistent with a safe global level of emissions. This limit is currently estimated to be 14.8 gigatons per year, or 2.3 tons per person. The current global per capita CO_2 emissions are 4.8 tons, about double the safe level.

Changing Relative Prices

In recent years, the relative price of manufactured goods has fallen, and commodity prices have risen. The rising price of food has created nutritional emergencies in some countries, which demand an immediate response. Looking forward, countries and international organizations need to be better prepared for sudden jumps in the price of essential commodities. It will be an ongoing feature of the global economy.

There is some evidence that growth in developing countries, principally China, has depressed the relative price of manufactured goods. This has raised the question of whether the growth strategies outlined in this report—strategies based on rapid job creation in labor-intensive export industries—will work in the future. We believe they will. With help from experts, we examined the so-called "adding up" problem: if many developing economies expanded their exports of labor-intensive manufactures, would the world market be able to absorb them all? We reached a positive conclusion: the growth of developing countries, at least in the early stages, will not be blocked by further rapid declines in the relative price of manufactured goods, in part because the growth of emerging markets will help fuel future demand.

Demographics

It is clear that the world population is aging rapidly, due to dramatically increased longevity combined with relatively low fertility rates. It is also clear that this trend will require many countries, both developed and developing, to change their pension and social security systems, and revise their expectations about retirement. What is not clear is whether aging will cause a slowdown in global growth and a narrowing of opportunities for developing countries. The answer depends on how quickly pension arrangements change and how quickly people adapt their behavior, by retiring later, for example. Timely adaptation will minimize the impact on global growth.

In a significant number of poorer countries, the demographics run directly counter to the global trend: high fertility; reduced longevity in some cases, due to diseases like HIV/AIDS; and an increasingly youthful population. This raises the danger of widespread youth unemployment. To avert this danger, countries need to grow faster. Migration, while not alone sufficient to solve the problem of youth unemployment, would help alleviate it. It would also benefit those host countries with an aging population. Well-managed long-term migration and well-supervised programs of temporary migration for work should be part of 21st century globalization.

Global Governance

A number of trends broached by the report demand a coordinated, multilateral response from the world's economies. These trends include the growing clout of developing countries, international financial spillovers, and the unbalanced and probably unsustainable pattern of saving and spending in the world economy.

Developing countries cannot grow without the support of the advanced economies. In particular, they need access to the open global trading system. They may also need some latitude to promote their exports, until their economies have matured and their competitive position has improved. The successful completion of the Doha round is substantively and symbolically important.

It will take time to develop a new "architecture" of institutions and rules to govern the world economy. In the meantime there will remain a mismatch between our deep interdependence and our limited capacity to coordinate our regulatory responses. This mismatch will create risks that countries will have to insure themselves against.

The recent success of many big developing countries raises an old question with renewed urgency: are there natural limits to growth? The rising price of commodities suggests that the world's endowment of natural resources may not easily accommodate the aspirations of poor countries. Likewise, the threat of global warming will grow as the developing world's industry expands.

We do not know if limits to growth exist, or how generous those limits will be. The answer will depend on our ingenuity and technology, on finding new ways to create goods and services that people value on a finite foundation of natural resources. This is likely to be the ultimate challenge of the coming century. Growth and poverty reduction in the future will depend on our ability to meet it.

Introduction

The Commission and Its Mandate

What do we know about economic growth? And what practical implications can policy makers draw from that knowledge? Those are both daunting questions, no easier to answer than they are to ignore. Since April 2006, they have guided the work of the Commission on Growth and Development, an independent group of policy makers, business leaders, and scholars, supported by the World Bank, the Hewlett Foundation, and the governments of Australia, Netherlands, Sweden, and the United Kingdom. Drawing on academic research, case histories, and practical experience, the Commission has weighed what is known about generating and sustaining fast growth in developing countries.

This assessment is meant to be useful to senior political and policy leaders, those whose job it is to craft a developing country's economic reforms. We hope it provides a framework within which policy makers can develop country-specific growth strategies of their own. We do not give policy makers all the answers, but we hope to help them ask the right questions. To this end, the majority of the members of the Commission are leaders from developing countries. Our intention is to share their experiences, priorities, successes, and failures with their peers and the next generation of leaders.

The Commission understands that growth is not an end in itself. It is instead a means to several ends that matter profoundly to individuals and societies. Growth is, above all, the surest way to free a society from poverty. Without it, a stark lack of material resources will tend to dominate everything else, narrowing people's horizons, consuming them in a daily struggle to get by, and depriving them of the chance to fulfill their potential. Prosperity, on the other hand, frees people to make choices, and allows a more equal distribution of opportunities. Human development, under-

---

Box 1: Growth and poverty

In the last 30 years absolute poverty has fallen substantially. This is almost entirely due to sustained growth. The fall is likely to continue because India is likely to grow at a fast pace for another 15 years, when it will catch up to where China is today, and China has another 600 million people in agriculture yet to move into more productive employment in urban areas.

In a very poor country, it is arithmetically impossible to reduce poverty without growth. There is no one to redistribute from. Conversely, if everyone is poor, growth will reduce poverty regardless of how it is distributed.

But some kinds of growth reduce poverty more effectively than others. The distribution of income can change as average incomes rise, becoming more or less equal. The expansion of smallholder farming, for example, cuts poverty quickly, raising the incomes of rural cultivators and reducing the price of the poor's food bill. Growth in labor-intensive manufacturing also raises the incomes of the poor. The expansion of capital-intensive mining industries, on the other hand, can result in jobless growth, making little impression on poverty.

One study shows that when average household incomes rise by 2 percent, poverty rates fall by about twice as much on average. But the range is wide, from as little as 1.2 percent to as much as 7 percent (95 percent confidence interval).[a]

Such studies look at spells of growth, some of them short-lived. This report is about sustained growth, lasting more than two decades. Over that timescale, growth almost always bites deeply into poverty. In some cases, it eliminates extreme poverty entirely. However growth starts, sustaining it will usually require mass job creation, raising the scarcity value of labor. As a result, wages rise, spreading the proceeds of growth more widely. In short, the most propoor growth is sustained growth.

This virtue of sustained growth is sometimes missed, because people confuse rising inequality with a failure to make progress against poverty. In economies without growth, a widening gap between rich and poor does indeed entail an increase in poverty. But in fast-growing economies, it is possible and quite normal for poverty to fall even as inequality rises.

The higher a country's average income level, the more complex is the relationship between growth and poverty reduction. In Latin America, for example, countries with incomes as high as $4,000 per head nevertheless contain large numbers of poor people. These impoverished populations are left behind by the rest of the economy, lacking access to formal jobs, capital markets, and public services. In such cases, growth is clearly not sufficient to reduce poverty. It may not be necessary either, because some progress can be made by redistributing income, assets, or access to services. But it is much easier to carry out a program of redistribution if the country is also growing. The proceeds of growth can then be redistributed without anyone's standard of living having to fall. That makes the politics of redistribution much easier. After all, the richer sections of society will settle for smaller gains in income more readily than they will accept a loss of income.

a. Ravallion, Martin. 2001. "Growth, Inequality, and Poverty: Looking Beyond Averages." Policy Research Working Paper 2558, World Bank, Washington, DC.

---

stood in its broadest sense, is both an "output" of growth and one of the most important inputs. We have focused on sustained growth because it creates options for individuals and societies that are difficult or impossible to achieve otherwise.

In the developed world, the great questions of growth and poverty are inseparable from debates about aid. Many believe foreign aid can help raise growth and fight poverty. They are probably right. Aid, however, is not the focus of this report. Donors can help governments in some poor countries by relaxing their financial limitations. But in many countries, the lack of aid dollars is not the binding constraint and in others it is only one constraint among many. It is not a substitute for leadership, good strategy, and effective implementation.

A great deal of aid is not intended to raise growth *per se*. It makes a contribution to the fight against disease and other social ills—worthy goals in themselves, whatever their effect on the economy. Other categories of aid do try to lift growth, by providing finance or expertise or both. If the logic of this report is compelling, it will be useful to these donors as they look for rewarding areas of investment.

The Commission asked distinguished academics and practitioners to assess the state of knowledge in a wide range of policy areas, from exchange rate intervention to school feeding programs. The result is a rich collection of papers, country case studies, and workshop deliberations available on the Commission's Web site.[1] In some cases there is widespread agreement. In others our knowledge is incomplete. In still others there are controversy and ongoing disagreement about the benefits and risks of a policy.

This report is not a summary of all those assessments, but a distillation of them, guided by the commissioners' own experience. Our goal has been to identify the key insights and policy levers that help countries raise and sustain the pace of growth and poverty reduction.

"The objective of growth is to lift the most vulnerable in society out of poverty. There is sufficient evidence to direct us as policy makers to those parts of the world where this has been done exceptionally well. And, for me, that is the light that emanates from the report."

—*Trevor Manuel*

The Organization of the Report

The report has four main parts. In the first, we review the 13 economies that have sustained, high growth in the postwar period. Their growth models had some common flavors: the strategic integration with the world economy; the mobility of resources, particularly labor; the high savings and investment rates; and a capable government committed to growth. The report goes on to describe the cast of mind and techniques of policy making that leaders will need if they are to emulate such a growth model. It concludes that their policy making will need to be patient, pragmatic, and experimental.

---

1 http://www.growthcommission.org.

In the second part, we lay out the ingredients a growth strategy might include. These range from public investment and exchange rate policies to land sales and redistribution. A list of ingredients is not enough to make a dish, of course, as Bob Solow, a Nobel Prize-winning economist and a member of the Commission, points out. We, however, refrain from offering policy makers a recipe, or growth strategy, to follow. This is because no single recipe exists. Timing and circumstance will determine how the ingredients should be combined, in what quantities, and in what sequence. In India, for example, policy makers must concentrate on infrastructure investment and improving the quality of education. In China, on the other hand, policy makers should try to wean the economy off exports and investment and give freer rein to consumption.

Formulating a full growth strategy, then, is not a job for this Commission but for a dedicated team of policy makers and economists, working on a single economy over time. Instead of a country-specific recipe, we offer some more general thoughts on the opportunities and constraints faced by nations in Sub-Saharan Africa, countries rich in resources, small states with fewer than 2 million people, and middle-income countries that have lost their economic momentum.

In the final part of the report, we discuss global trends that are beyond the control of any single developing-country policy maker. Global warming is one example; the surge in protectionist sentiment another; the rise of commodity prices a third. In addition, we discuss the aging of the world population and the potential dangers of America's external deficit. These trends are new enough that the 13 high-growth economies of the postwar period did not have to face them. The question is whether they now make it impossible for other countries to emulate that postwar success.

The developing countries today have a collective importance in the world economy that is impossible to ignore. They leave a sizable imprint on commodity prices, inflation, capital flows, and greenhouse gas emissions, to name just some of the ripple effects. Their collective importance has, however, yet to be fully reflected in the few international institutions that help steward the world economy. This should change. The developing world has benefited enormously from the global economy and contributed a great deal to it. Now their policy makers need to assume a bigger role in managing it.

PART 1

Sustained, High Growth in the Postwar Period

What Is Growth?

Gross domestic product (GDP) is a familiar but remarkable statistic. It is an astonishing feat of statistical compression, reducing the restless endeavor and bewildering variety of a national economy into a single number, which can increase over time. China's GDP grew by 11.9 percent in 2007, America's may not grow at all in 2008. Both of those terse statistical statements sum up world-changing developments, which will attract vast volumes of commentary and explanation. Few other statistics in the social sciences are as expressive.

A growing GDP is evidence of a society getting its collective act together. As its economy grows, a society becomes more tightly organized, more densely interwoven. A growing economy is one in which energies are better directed; resources better deployed; techniques mastered, then advanced. It is not just about making money.

Economic growth is a recent phenomenon in human history. It began with the industrial revolution in Britain at the end of the 18th century. "It is impossible to contemplate the progress of manufactures in Great Britain within the last thirty years without wonder and astonishment," wrote Patrick Colquhoun, a Scottish merchant, in 1814. This progress spread to Europe and North America in the 19th century, accelerating as it traveled. In the 20th century, particularly in the second half, it spread and accelerated again.

Mr. Colquhoun attributed the progress he saw to "ingenious machinery, invigorated by capital and skill." Today's economists account for growth with much the same triple formula of technology, capital, and human capital. But these are only the proximate causes of growth. Its deeper roots draw on advances in science, finance, trade, education, medicine, public health, and government, to name but a few of the factors in play.

Over the past two centuries, what we now call the global economy has expanded in fits and starts. Interrupted by the slump of the 1930s, it was rebuilt in the 1940s, when the institutional foundations of today's world economy (the General Agreement on Tariffs and Trade, the precursor of the World Trade Organization; the International Monetary Fund; the World Bank; and the United Nations and its diverse agencies) were laid. Globalization has since proceeded apace, aided by legislation (the lowering of tariffs and quotas and the relaxation of capital controls) and innovation (the declining cost of transport and communication).

This renaissance of the world economy helps to explain an uptick in world growth since the latter half of the 20th century (see figure 1). As the world economy has opened and integrated, technology and know-how have flowed more easily to developing countries. Latecomers can assimilate new techniques much more quickly than the pioneering economies can invent them. That is why poorer countries can "catch up" with richer ones.

Figure 1 Evolution of Global and Per Capita GDP in the Last 2,000 Years

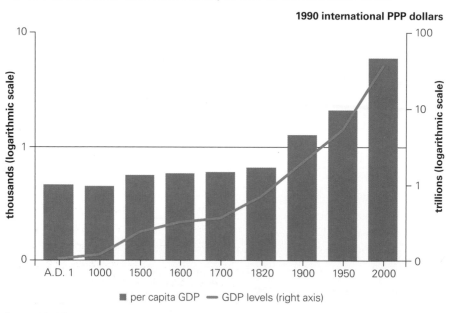

Source: Maddison, Angus. 2007. *Contours of the World Economy, 1–2030 AD.* Oxford, UK: Oxford University Press.

Note: PPP = purchasing power parity.

The lessons that countries import are not only technological. Both China and then India reformed their closed, heavily regulated economies, motivated in part by the force of international example. These epic *voltes face* also help to explain why global growth has increased in recent decades. It was probably no harder to reverse the policies of India and China than to reform the policies of Mauritius and Vietnam. But political breakthroughs in vast places benefit a much greater proportion of the globe.

This accelerating growth has created new challenges. The first is a clear divergence in incomes within and between countries. Of the roughly 6 billion people on the planet, about 65 percent live in high-income or high-growth economies, up from less than a fifth 30 years ago. The remaining 2 billion people live in countries with stagnating, or even declining, incomes. The world population is projected to increase by 3 billion people by 2050. Unfortunately, 2 billion of this extra population will live in countries that are currently enjoying little or no growth. Thus, if these trends persist, the proportion of the world population living in low-growth environments might increase.

The second challenge is environmental. The quickened growth of world GDP has put new pressure on the planet's ecology and climate. This strain may ultimately threaten the growth environment of the last 200 years.[2] If an economy fails to grow, man's efforts to better himself become a scramble for a bigger share of a fixed amount of resources. Ecological stress quickly becomes social and political. Some of these pressures and their implications are discussed in part 4 of the report.

The 13 Success Stories

As a point of departure we review the cases of high, sustained growth in the postwar period. Thirteen economies qualify: Botswana; Brazil; China; Hong Kong, China; Indonesia; Japan; the Republic of Korea; Malaysia; Malta; Oman; Singapore; Taiwan, China; and Thailand. Two other countries, India and Vietnam, may be on their way to joining this group. It is to be hoped other countries will emerge soon.

These cases demonstrate that fast, sustained growth is possible—after all, 13 economies have achieved it. They also show that it is not easy—after all, *only* 13 economies have ever done it. Indeed, some people view these cases as "economic miracles," events impossible to explain and unlikely to be repeated. This report takes exception to that view. There is much to learn from outliers. Paul Romer, a leading growth theorist and a member

---

2   See Martin Wolf on the possibility of returning to the zero-sum environment that characterized the pregrowth period, with the attendant risks of conflict. Wolf, Martin. 2007. "The Dangers of Living in a Zero-Sum World Economy." *The Financial Times*, December 19.

of the Commission's working group, reminds us that when Japan grew at this pace, commentators said it was a special case propelled by postwar recovery. When the four East Asian tigers (Hong Kong, China; Taiwan, China; Singapore; and Korea) matched it, skeptics said it was only possible because they were so small. When China surpassed them, people said it was only because China was so big.

In truth, the sample is remarkably diverse (see table 1). The familiar Asian examples may dominate the list, but every other region of the developing world (Africa, Latin America, the Middle East, and emerging Europe) is also represented. Some of the countries are rich in natural resources (Botswana, Brazil, Indonesia, Malaysia, Oman, Thailand); the remainder are not. The sample includes one country with a population well over 1 billion (China), and another with a population well below 500,000 (Malta).

Perhaps more intriguing is how differently the success stories end. Six of the economies (Hong Kong, China; Japan; Korea; Malta; Singapore; and Taiwan, China) continued to grow all the way to high-income levels. But several of the others lost some or all of their growth momentum long before catching the leading economies. The most striking example is Brazil, where fast economic growth petered out around the time of the second oil shock in 1979 and has yet to resume (see box 2).

The 13 economies each, then, have their idiosyncrasies. But it would be wrong to conclude that they defy generalization, or that there is no point in learning about their growth paths because the lessons cannot be applied at home. That was not the attitude the countries themselves took. Policy mak-

Table 1 13 Success Stories of Sustained, High Growth

Economy	Period of high growth**	Per capita income at the beginning and 2005***	
Botswana	1960–2005	210	3,800
Brazil	1950–1980	960	4,000
China	1961–2005	105	1,400
Hong Kong, China*	1960–1997	3,100	29,900
Indonesia	1966–1997	200	900
Japan*	1950–1983	3,500	39,600
Korea, Rep. of*	1960–2001	1,100	13,200
Malaysia	1967–1997	790	4,400
Malta*	1963–1994	1,100	9,600
Oman	1960–1999	950	9,000
Singapore*	1967–2002	2,200	25,400
Taiwan, China*	1965–2002	1,500	16,400
Thailand	1960–1997	330	2,400

Source: World Bank, World Development Indicators.

*Economies that have reached industrialized countries' per capita income levels.
**Period in which GDP growth was 7 percent per year or more.
***In constant US$ of 2000.

Box 2: Brazil's slowdown

Brazil was one of the first countries to achieve sustained, high growth (its run began in 1950) and the first to lose its momentum (in 1980). At first glance, Brazil's case sits uneasily beside the other 12 on our list. Unlike those countries, it is best known for a strategy of "import substitution," sheltering its domestic industries so they could compete for the home market against foreign rivals.

During its first phase of import substitution, however, Brazil in fact succeeded in diversifying its exports, branching out from coffee into light manufacturing with the help of foreign direct investment. Exports as a percentage of GDP more than doubled from 5 percent in the early-1950s to about 12 percent in the early 1980s, even as coffee's share of exports fell dramatically. Brazil also had the twin advantages of a sizable domestic market and abundant agricultural resources. These two endowments allowed it to reach very high growth rates despite a modest engagement with the world economy.

Why did it slow down? The causes are hard to disentangle, just as the slowdown has been hard to reverse. Brazil's problems began after the first oil shock in 1973, which left the country suffering from inflation and an overhang of debt. In response, the government in 1974 turned further inward. It began a "second phase" of import substitution, which went beyond light manufacturing to promote heavy industries and capital goods production, a strategy that was heavily dependent on the recycling of petrodollars. When dollar interest rates spiked after 1979, Brazil plunged into a debt and high-inflation crisis from which it took more than a decade to emerge. In the process, Brazil's exports declined from 12 percent of GDP in the early 1980s to 6 percent in the mid-1990s, losing nearly all of the ground they had gained in the high-growth period.

---

ers learned by example; case studies had a pronounced influence; demonstration effects were surprisingly important. It is said that Deng Xiaoping was strongly influenced by his first encounters with Singapore and New York City, on a visit to the United Nations.

A close look at the 13 cases reveals five striking points of resemblance (see figure 2):

1. They fully exploited the world economy
2. They maintained macroeconomic stability
3. They mustered high rates of saving and investment
4. They let markets allocate resources
5. They had committed, credible, and capable governments

1. The global economy

During their periods of fast growth, these 13 economies all made the most of the global economy. This is their most important shared characteristic and the central lesson of this report. Sustained growth at this pace was not possible before 1950. It became feasible only because the world economy became more open and more tightly integrated.[3] The global economy is still

---

3 As Barry Bosworth of the Brookings Institution has noted, this opening is not just about cutting tariffs, but also about expanding the range of goods that can be traded and included in multilateral trade negotiations.

Figure 2 The Common Characteristics of High, Sustained Growth

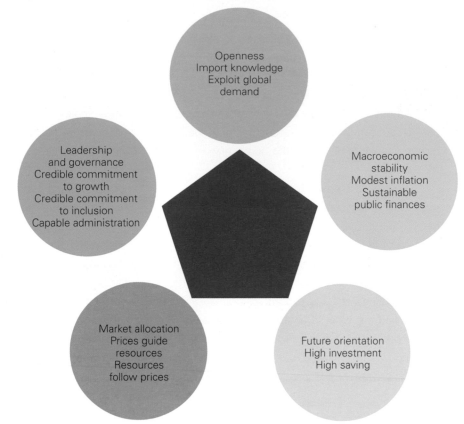

Openness
Import knowledge
Exploit global
demand

Leadership
and governance
Credible commitment
to growth
Credible commitment
to inclusion
Capable administration

Macroeconomic
stability
Modest inflation
Sustainable
public finances

Market allocation
Prices guide
resources
Resources
follow prices

Future orientation
High investment
High saving

a work in progress, of course, but its effects have already been dramatic. Properly exploited for the benefit of all citizens, it is one of the most powerful weapons against poverty.

The high-growth countries benefited in two ways. One, they imported ideas, technology, and know-how from the rest of the world. Two, they exploited global demand, which provided a deep, elastic market for their goods. The inflow of knowledge dramatically increased the economy's productive potential; the global market provided the demand necessary to fulfill it. To put it very simply, they imported what the rest of the world knew, and exported what it wanted.

Knowledge

It is easier to learn something than it is to invent it. That is why advanced economies do not grow (and cannot grow) at rates of 7 percent or more, and why lagging economies can catch up. To take an early example: the textiles industry of Osaka eclipsed the mills of Lancashire by borrowing, assimilating, and improving British designs and techniques. The façade of the Osaka Spinning Company, established in 1883, was even built from imported Lancashire red brick.[4]

There are many channels through which knowledge can pass to a developing economy. One is foreign direct investment (FDI). Malaysia, for example, has attracted multinationals to its three electronics clusters—in Penang, the Klang Valley, and Johore—where they enjoy tax holidays and other privileges.[5] Multinationals bring production technologies, an understanding of the global market, and an ability to manage international supply chains. Japan and Korea were historically much less open to FDI, but they did import and improve upon technology from outside. Japan's Sony, for example, surpassed America's RCA in the market for small radios, using technology it had licensed from the American company itself.

Demand

The global economy also provides a large, relatively stable market for the goods of developing countries. In the 1950s, some economists fell prey to "export pessimism." They assumed that the more goods the developing world sold on global markets, the lower the price they would fetch. This thesis may or may not have been true for primary products and commodities. But it did not hold for the manufactured goods in which many of our 13 success stories developed a comparative advantage. In most cases, their potential output was small relative to the size of the world market.[6] This gave them scope to specialize, raise productivity dramatically, and expand their output manifold. The four tigers, for example, increased their manufactured exports from $4.6 billion (in 2000 dollars) in 1962 to $715 billion in 2004. If there was any small decline in price, it was overwhelmed by the vigorous growth in sales.

This is one reason why inward-looking growth strategies quickly falter. Domestic demand is no substitute for this expansive global market. In a poor country, the home market is small and therefore relatively "inelastic." For sales to rise, prices have to fall. Size is not the only problem. The pattern of domestic spending may not correspond well to the strengths of domestic supply. What home consumers want to buy may not match what home producers are best at making. Since specialization is limited by the extent of the market, home markets give an economy less scope to specialize in its areas of comparative advantage.

"In the 1950s Korea pursued a policy of import substitution. Growth was only 2–3 percent. But in the early 1960s, Korea totally changed to an outward-oriented strategy, emphasizing trade. This jump-started our growth to over 7 percent, sustained over a long period."

—Han Duck-soo

---

4   Saxonhouse, Gary. 1974. "A Tale of Japanese Technological Diffusion in the Meiji Period." *The Journal of Economic History* 34 (1): 149–65.

5   Yusof, Zainal Aznam, and Bhattasali, Deepak. 2007. "Economic Growth and Development in Malaysia: Policy Making and Leadership." Case Study, Commission on Growth and Development.

6   Two exceptions may be China in manufacturing and India in services.

2. Macroeconomic stability

Macroeconomic volatility and unpredictability damage private sector investment, and hence, growth. During their most successful periods, the 13 high-growth cases avoided the worst of this turbulence.

Their quick expansion was accompanied, from time to time, by moderately high inflation. Korea, for example, had double-digit inflation rates for most of the 1970s; China's inflation peaked at about 24 percent in 1994. But prices were stable enough not to scramble market signals, cloud the view of long-term investors, or deter savers from entrusting their wealth to banks.

Governments were also fiscally responsible. Many ran budget deficits for extended periods; some nursed high ratios of debt to GDP. But this public debt did not get out of hand, not least because the economy grew faster than the stock of public liabilities.

3. Future orientation

This macroeconomic stability set the stage for their third characteristic: they all mustered high rates of saving and investment, not least public investment in infrastructure. They were all "future-oriented," forgoing consumption in the present in pursuit of a higher level of income in the future.

In the mid-1970s, Southeast Asia and Latin America had similar savings rates. Twenty years later, the Asian rate was about 20 percentage points higher. China has saved more than a third of its national income every year for the past 25 years. This saving has been accompanied by prodigious rates of domestic investment.

In a paper written for the Commission, Peter Montiel of Williams College and Luis Serven of the World Bank catalog some of the possible reasons for East Asia's thrift.[7] The region benefited from favorable demography. With fewer dependents to take care of, working-age adults had more scope to put money aside. Macroeconomic stability also helped. Thailand's saving rate rose quickly in the 1980s, for example, thanks to tighter government budgets. As mentioned, these countries also mostly avoided high and unpredictable inflation, which arbitrarily redistributes wealth from savers to debtors and discourages people from holding financial assets.

Some countries employed more direct measures to enforce thrift. In 1955, Singapore established a mandatory saving scheme, the Central Provident Fund, which collects contributions from wages that are primarily saved until retirement, although some withdrawals for medical and housing have been permitted. Malaysia has a similar system. Both countries, as well as Japan and Korea, also had postal saving systems, which catered to the needs of small savers. Their financial systems were, by contrast, less ready

"The three "dos" for growth that I care most about in the report are economic openness, social inclusiveness, and effective governments. The message can be spelled out equally well in three "don'ts": inwardness, exclusion, and bloated governments—a recipe for stagnation."

—Edmar Bacha

---

7   Montiel, Peter, and Serven, Luis. 2008. "Real Exchange Rates, Saving, and Growth: Is There a Link?" Background Paper, Commission on Growth and Development.

to extend consumer credit. By making it harder to borrow, they may have made it easier to save.

4. Market allocation

The 20th century saw many experiments with alternatives to markets. They were all conclusive failures. It therefore seems safe to say that markets are a necessary part of the economic structure in order to achieve and sustain growth.

The high-growth economies all relied on a functioning market system, which provided price signals, decentralized decision making, and incentives to supply whatever was in demand. Countries varied in the strength and clarity of their property rights. But in all cases, firms and entrepreneurs felt they had enough of a claim on their assets to invest heavily in them.

In Hong Kong, China, the administration was famously laissez faire. Other governments in our list were more hands-on, intervening with tax breaks, subsidized credit, directed lending and other such measures. These interventions may have helped them to discover their comparative advantage—revealing how best to deploy their endowments of labor and capital. But they did not defy their comparative advantage, as Justin Yifu Lin, the chief economist of the World Bank, has put it. This distinction is conceptually subtle, but economically consequential.

An economy's endowment of labor, natural resources, and capital dictates its comparative advantage. But this mandate is very broad. The crowded, coastal economies of East Asia, for example, had a comparative advantage in labor-intensive manufacturing. But what line of labor-intensive manufacturing, precisely? Using what techniques? Those answers they had to discover for themselves through trial and error. This process of "self-discovery" may have been helped along by the government's hand.[8] What was not helpful were government efforts to promote heavy industry, before accumulating the capital required to make it viable.

Resource mobility and structural transformation

A country's comparative advantage will evolve over time. In any period of fast growth, capital, and especially, labor moves rapidly from sector to sector, industry to industry. This mobility of resources was a feature of all the 13 high-growth cases. Governments did not resist (although they may have tempered) the market forces that pulled people into the urban areas or destroyed some jobs, while creating others. In Malaysia, for example, agriculture's share of employment fell from 40 percent in 1975 to about 15 percent in 2000. Only a quarter of Malaysia's people lived in cities in 1957, the year of its independence; by 2005, 63 percent did. Even in China, where

"Government provides the environment for growth, but it is the private sector that invests and creates wealth for the people."
—Goh Chok Tong

---

8   Hausmann, Ricardo, and Rodrik, Dani. 2003. "Economic Development as Self-Discovery." *Journal of Development Economics* 72: 603–33.

the household registration system placed some restrictions on mobility, vast shifts of population have taken place.

Economies do not grow smoothly and evenly, maintaining their shape as they increase their size. Instead, fast-growing economies go through a tumultuous process of creative destruction, breaking into new industries even as they abandon their traditional industrial strongholds. The challenge that each of the 13 governments faced was how to shield people from the worst of this tumult, without retarding the economy in the process.

5. Leadership and governance

Growth is about more than economics. It also requires committed, credible, and capable governments. "[I]n the long run it does not pay to build an economic mansion on a foundation of political sand," writes Benjamin Mkapa, former president of Tanzania, in a paper written for the Commission.[9] The high-growth economies typically built their prosperity on sturdy political foundations.

Their policy makers understood that growth does not just happen. It must be consciously chosen as an overarching goal by a country's leadership. In Singapore, for example, the pursuit of growth has served as an organizing principle of the country's politics for the past 40 years, according to a recent speech by Senior Minister Goh Chok Tong, a member of the Commission. The government and other institutions have constantly sought to anticipate the actions required to sustain the economy's momentum.

Does that make Singapore unusual? After all, most political leaders advertise their commitment to economic development. But in their choices, if not their words, many governments prize political tranquility over the economic upheaval that growth can entail. Others carry out plausible economic reforms for their own sake. If growth does not ensue, they do not experiment with something else; they simply declare victory and go home.

In the fast-growing economies, by contrast, policy makers understood that successful development entails a decades-long commitment, and a fundamental bargain between the present and the future. Even at very high growth rates of 7–10 percent it takes decades for a country to make the leap from low to relatively high incomes (see figure 3).

During this long period of transition, citizens must forgo consumption today in return for higher standards of living tomorrow. This bargain will be accepted only if the country's policy makers communicate a credible vision of the future and a strategy for getting there. They must be trusted as stewards of the economy and their promises of future rewards must be believed.

"I think leadership matters, but I don't mean just the top leader. I think you also need a team that knows what the right policies are and has the skills, or is able to contract the skills, to help implement those policies."

—Ngozi N. Okonjo-Iweala

---

9   Mkapa, Benjamin. 2007. "Leadership for Growth, Development and Poverty Reduction: An African Viewpoint and Experience." Case Study, Commission on Growth and Development.

Figure 3 Transitions to Higher Incomes

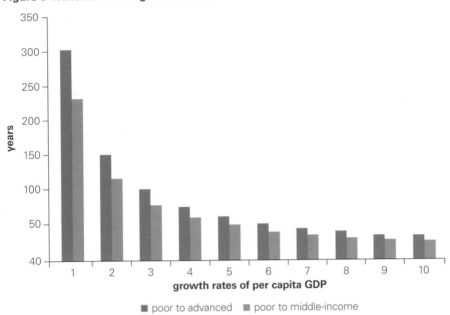

■ poor to advanced ■ poor to middle-income

Their promise must also be inclusive, leaving citizens confident that they and their children will share in the benefits. In Botswana, for example, Seretse Khama handed over diamond mining rights from his own tribe to the government, which gave every tribe in Botswana a bigger stake in the state's success.[10] Other governments forged an implicit or explicit social contract in support of growth, offering health, education, and sometimes redistribution. These contracts were kept, if not in detail, then at least in spirit. Absent this kind of political foundation, sustaining the policies that promote growth is very difficult if not impossible.

Such leadership requires patience and a long planning horizon. In several cases, fast-growing economies were overseen by a single-party government that could expect to remain in power for decades to come. In a multiparty democracy, on the other hand, governments typically look no further than the next election. But democracies can nonetheless preside over remarkable passages of growth. Today's India is the most prominent example. But Ireland and Australia also provide some instructive lessons.

Australia's Productivity Commission was established by an act of parliament in 1998, although it can trace its roots back 30 years. An independent state agency, it regularly evaluates government regulations and microeconomic policies, analyzes Australia's long-term growth prospects, and helps bring people together to craft proposals for reform. The Irish Social Partnership, which arose out of the country's economic stagnation in the 1980s,

"Reforms can be costly—they can withdraw from the political capital of governments. So after some achievements, governments may start to relax or enjoy the status quo. But what matters is sustainable efforts, not the ups and downs or ons and offs of reforms."

—Mahmoud Mohieldin

---

10 Acemoglu, Daron, and Robinson, James. 2007. "The Role of Institutions in Growth and Development." Background Paper, Commission on Growth and Development.

brings employers, unions, and the government together every three years to rethink and renegotiate the nation's economic strategy. Once these deliberations are ratified, they become the framework for policy making for the next three years.

These latter cases show that democracies can be surprisingly farsighted. Rival political parties can, for example, agree on a bipartisan growth strategy, which they each promise to follow when it is their turn in power. Even if a formal pact is never made, a successful growth strategy, commanding the confidence of the public, may outlast the government that introduced it.

Committed to the goal of high growth, governments should be pragmatic in their pursuit of it. The policy makers who succeeded in sustaining high growth were prepared to try, fail, and learn. Singapore, for example, did not turn outward until it had first tried turning inward, encouraging domestic firms to compete with industrial imports. In China, Deng Xiaoping reportedly described his approach as crossing the river by feeling for the stones—an oft-repeated phrase in China.

The Art of Policy Making

It is relatively easy to identify the shared characteristics of the high-growth cases and easy to appreciate their collective importance. But it is hard to know how to replicate these characteristics. Some of them are the outcome of innumerable decisions and interactions by firms, households, and offi-

---

Box 3: Reform teams

The business of "feeling for the stones" in fast-growing economies was often carried out by highly qualified technocrats in small, dedicated "reform teams"[a]. Singapore had its Economic Development Board, Korea its Economic Planning Board, and Japan its Ministry of Trade and Industry.

Reform teams were not burdened with administrative duties, but they were given direct access to the top of the government. Malaysia's Economic Planning Unit reported directly to the prime minister. Taiwan, China's Council for U.S. Aid, which began in 1948 and evolved into the Council for Economic Planning and Development, reported directly to the president. Indeed, several future heads of government sprang from their ranks: the second chairman of the Council later became president of the country.

From this unique position—ensconced in the government, but distanced from day-to-day administrative burdens and immediate political demands[b]—the reform teams helped coordinate the government's efforts and overcome administrative opposition and inertia.

Although technocrats unchecked by political forces can fail to balance economic with political and social concerns, political forces unchecked by technocratic knowledge can be disruptive.

---

a. Criscuolo, Alberto, and Palmade, Vincent. 2008. "Reform Teams: How the Most Successful Reformers Organized Themselves." Public Policy for the Private Sector Note 318, World Bank, Washington, DC.

b. Evans, Peter. 1995. *Embedded Autonomy: States and Industrial Transformation.* Princeton, NJ: Princeton University Press.

---

cials. Some are the result of evolution, not design. None is a straightforward policy.

For example, the success stories show that high, sustained growth requires an impressive saving rate. But what should governments do to promote thrift? Should they restrict credit, mandate saving, or raise taxes? The historical record shows that growth requires broadly stable prices, a currency that is not debauched by hyperinflation. But does that mean the central bank should be made formally independent? It is also clear that successful economies learned quickly from the rest of the world, assimilating new techniques. But how can policy makers help an economy to learn?

In the context of a developed country, economists prescribe policies with some measure of confidence. Some advisers offer prescriptions to poorer countries with the same level of conviction. They argue that developing economies are just like advanced economies, only poorer.

But in recent decades, economists have acquired a deeper appreciation of the underlying institutions that make mature markets work. These institutions define property rights, enforce contracts, convey information, and bridge informational gaps between buyers and sellers. These institutions and capabilities may not be fully formed in a developing economy. Indeed, the immaturity of these institutions is synonymous with underdevelopment. That makes it harder to predict how an economy will respond to, say, the removal of a tariff or the sale of a public asset.

Uncertain about how to model developing economies, we also suspect that the correct model changes over time. A fast-growing economy is a moving target. Often markets and institutions co-evolve, responding to the constraints and the demands one places on the other. Land registries, for example, emerge only after land becomes scarce. Accountancy evolves as and when the capital markets demand it.

This makes life doubly difficult for policy makers. It is hard to know how the economy will respond to a policy, and the right answer in the present moment may not apply in the future. Today's bad policies are often yesterday's good policies, applied for too long. Governing a growing economy is not a static challenge. It is more akin to a long voyage undertaken with incomplete and sometimes inaccurate charts.[11]

The Role of Government

What then should governments do? What is the optimal size of the state and what are its proper responsibilities? More ink has been spilled on that question than any other in development. It is a recurring theme of this report and the debates that preceded it.

"Markets and governments work differently at different stages of development— their structure, their functions, their goals all change. There are phases in which governments substitute for markets and phases in which market institutions develop."

—*Zhou Xiaochuan*

---

11 Four decades ago, independent Singapore embarked on an uncertain journey. Unemployment was high, industry nonexistent, and the future looked bleak. Prime Minister Lee Kuan Yew wrote of that day, "I started out with great trepidation on a journey along an unmarked road to an unknown destination."

One response is to argue that governments should do as little as possible. "That government is best which governs least," as the motto goes. Fifteen years ago, much of the discussion of government shared this presumption in favor of smaller government and freer markets. Its policy conclusions are captured in the phrase: "Stabilize, privatize, and liberalize."

While there is some merit in what lies behind this prescription, it is an extremely incomplete statement of the problem. It is true that bloated government should not crowd out the private sector; regulation should not be excessive; the economy should be open to trade and competition; and private investors should be free to earn a remunerative return. The injunction to roll back the state was also motivated in part by concerns about the motivation and competence of government. If government's role is defined too broadly, it may not have the capacity to perform such an expansive array of functions. Or it may misuse its broader mandate, pursuing goals other than growth and widespread prosperity, such as the welfare of vested interests.

But our view of effective government is somewhat different. The issues of competence and motivation cannot be dismissed. But they cannot be answered by simply writing government out of the script. Our model of developing economies is too primitive at this stage to make it wise to pre-define what governments should do. Numerous country case studies suggest that its role evolves over time as its own capabilities and those of the private sector mature. Our motto then would follow Sir Arthur Lewis, the great development economist, who observed that "[G]overnments may fail either because they do too little, or because they do too much."[12]

Some countries, for example, suffer from too little public investment; others, from too much government regulation. Some suffer from both problems simultaneously. In India, for example, the first priority in the 1990s was for the government to do less, dismantling the excesses of the license-and-permit Raj. Now the government is trying to do more, making up for years of underinvestment in public infrastructure.[13]

A preoccupation with the size of government can also distract attention from its effectiveness. History is littered with instructive examples. After the Great Depression, economists came to understand that America's fledgling central bank made the slump much worse. They could have argued for sharply limiting the powers and activities of the central bank, and some did. But others focused on how to help central banks do their job more effectively: how to free them from harmful political constraints, establish their credibility, and improve their tools and techniques. To us, this second approach seems more promising in developing countries. The task is to

"If I were to make a provocative statement, I would say that the prevalence of the first-best, optimal policy approach, which implies an excess of orthodoxy, leads to sub-optimal growth performance. That's a pretty strong statement."

—Alejandro Foxley

---

12 Lewis, Arthur. 1955. *The Theory of Economic Growth*. London: George Allen & Unwin.
13 See Montek Singh Ahluwalia (the Deputy Chairman of India's Planning Commission and a member of the Commission) in an interview in *The McKinsey Quarterly*, October 2007.

improve the effectiveness of government institutions rather than stripping them of their tasks.

It seems to us that the correct response to uncertainty is not paralysis but experiment. Governments should not do nothing, out of a fear of failure. They should test policies, and be quick to learn from failure. If they suffer a misstep, they should try something else, not plunge ahead or retreat to the shore.

These experiments should, however, be cautious. Each step should be weighed to generate the greatest amount of information about the economy for the least cost, should the policy prove to be a misstep. When they choose policies, governments should ask themselves, what is the worst that could happen? Small experiments are usually less damaging, should they fail, than big ones. Risk management is an important aspect of policy formation in developing countries.

China offers examples of such cautious policy making. Its initial reforms in 1978 freed farmers to sell any surplus produce, over and above government production quotas, on the open market. They responded much as microeconomic theory would predict. Prices rose, farm output soared, and farmers' lives improved. On the other hand, Chinese reformers have been careful not to copy macroeconomic policies from advanced economies. They knew that the economy early in the reform period would not respond to macroeconomic variables, like interest rates, in the way predicted by advanced country models.

Some question this deliberate, step-by-step gradualism. In some cases, "bad times make good policies." Crises, which can upset the stable configuration of political forces, sometimes provide an opening to implement major reform packages that would otherwise be blocked. However, there are possibly as many examples of crises leading to bad choices, as there are cases of crises leading to good ones. In short, crises may remove obstacles to a sound growth strategy, but they cannot ensure that a sound strategy will indeed be chosen. In this context, leadership and influential and enlightened technocrats play an enormously important role.

"Pragmatism and gradualism are different. In Indonesia, reforms have been pragmatic, willing to accommodate political and social reality. But they have not been gradual. When the economy was growing well, complacency set in. It was only when fortunes reversed that the reformers were able to move, and then they had to move quickly."

—*Dr. Boediono*

PART 2

The Policy Ingredients of Growth Strategies

We do not know the sufficient conditions for growth. We can characterize the successful economies of the postwar period, but we cannot name with certainty the factors that sealed their success, or the factors they could have succeeded without. It would be preferable if it were otherwise.

Nonetheless, the commissioners have a keen sense of the policies that probably matter— the policies that will make a material difference to a country's chances of sustaining high growth, even if they do not provide a rock-solid guarantee.

Just as we cannot say this list is sufficient, we cannot say for sure that all the ingredients are necessary. Countries have grown, for a time, on the back of a much shorter set of policies than this. But we suspect that over the course of 10 or 20 years of fast growth, all of these ingredients will matter. Low inflation, for example, will not compensate for poor education or rickety infrastructure. To sustain growth over a long period, a set of things needs to come together. Doing some subset of them may produce beneficial results. But the items the policy maker neglects will eventually haunt the economy's progress.

A list of ingredients is not a recipe, and our list does not constitute a growth strategy. We identify possible constraints on the economy's performance. A fully fledged growth strategy would identify which of these constraints demands immediate attention and which can be deferred. It would

"We shouldn't slip into the mistake of equating something useful, like financial-sector development or anything else, with a sufficient condition for growth."

—Michael Spence

specify what to do, when, and how much money, expertise and political capital to devote where. Given limited resources, governments should focus their effort in those areas with the highest incremental payoff to growth. But setting these priorities requires subtle judgments made with limited information. It is not a job for this Commission, but for a "reform team" of applied economists and policy makers with a deep knowledge of a particular country's circumstances. Nonetheless, such an exercise would surely benefit from paying close attention to the policies listed here. Our framework may not provide policy makers with all the answers, but we hope at least to help them ask the right questions.

The policies we explore fall into several loose categories: accumulation, innovation, allocation, stabilization, and inclusion.

The first set of policies on the list falls into the category of "accumulation." It includes strong public investment, which helps the economy to accumulate the infrastructure and skills it needs to grow quickly. The next group of measures promotes "innovation" and "imitation." They help an economy to learn to do new things—venturing into unfamiliar export industries for example—and to do things in new ways.

In any successful period of growth, relative prices have a lot of work to do, attracting investment into certain industries, deterring it from others. Thus, the third set of policies concerns the "allocation" of capital and, especially, labor. They allow prices to guide resources and resources to respond to prices. This microeconomics cannot unfold if it is rudely interrupted by debt crises or wild fluctuations in the general price level. The fourth group of policies therefore ensures the "stabilization" of the macroeconomy, safeguarding against slumps, insolvency, and runaway inflation.

We also recommend a set of policies to promote "inclusion." The commissioners prize equity and equality of opportunity for their own sake. But they also recognize that if a growth strategy brings all classes and regions of a society along with it, no group will seek to derail it.

High Levels of Investment

Strong, enduring growth requires high rates of investment. By investing resources, rather than consuming them, economies make a trade-off between present and future standards of living. That trade-off is quite steep. If the sustained, high-growth cases are any guide, it appears that overall investment rates of 25 percent of GDP or above are needed, counting both public and private expenditures (see figure 4). They often invested at least another 7–8 percent of GDP in education, training, and health (also counting public and private spending), although this is not treated as investment in the national accounts.

"Checklists of reforms are not helpful. The implicit message to policy makers is: if price control is difficult, why not do education? There is no element of strategy in that approach, no sense of the time lags or horizons involved."

—Ngozi N. Okonjo-Iweala

Figure 4 Percentage of GDP, Investment Rates by Growth 13, 1971–2004

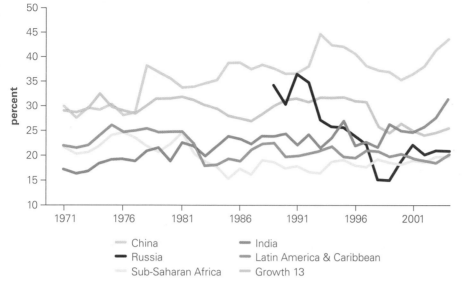

China · India · Russia · Latin America & Caribbean · Sub-Saharan Africa · Growth 13

Source: World Bank.

Infrastructure

In fast-growing Asia, public investment in infrastructure accounts for 5–7 percent of GDP or more. In China, Thailand, and Vietnam, total infrastructure investment exceeds 7 percent of GDP. History suggests this is the right order of magnitude for high and sustained growth, although it is difficult to be precise.

The data on public investment in infrastructure is surprisingly patchy. The numbers one can find suggest that spending is disturbingly low on average. Many developing countries invest on the order of 2 percent of GDP, or less—and this is reflected in their growth rate.

These two deficiencies—the shortage of data and the lack of spending—may be connected. What gets attention gets measured and what gets measured gets attention. Macroeconomic data are collected mostly for the purpose of stabilizing the economy in the short run. For that purpose, what matters is the overall level of government spending—the distinction between current outlays and capital investment is of little importance. But for growth, the distinction is essential.

Too often, both the composition and the size of public spending constitute a victory of the short run over the long run. Immediate claims for current spending—to pay wages, benefit politically powerful groups, or protect the population against declines in consumption—take away resources from what is important for the longer term. If the government's budget is too large, it can also crowd out private investment in the future. Spending, after

"International financial institutions, the IMF in particular, have tended to see public investment as a short-term stabilization issue, and failed to grasp its long-term growth consequences. If low-income countries are stuck in a low-level equilibrium, then putting constraints on their infrastructure spending may ensure they never take off."

—Montek Singh Ahluwalia

all, must be financed by taxes, fees, or inflation, all of which deprive the private sector of resources it might otherwise have invested in growth.

On the other hand, public spending on infrastructure—roads, ports, airports, and power—crowds private investment in. It expands investment opportunities and raises the return to private investment. By paving the way for new industries to emerge, it is also a crucial aid to structural transformation and export diversification.

Telecommunications infrastructure (and the pricing of services) is of particular importance. Telecommunications plays a variety of crucial roles in the public and private sector. It can aid education, transparency initiatives, and the delivery of government services. It can also raise productivity by disseminating price information to farmers, fishermen, and other producers. Telecommunications promotes widespread access to financial services. It also enables trade in services (a rapidly growing area of commerce) and links to global supply chains.

Given the great importance of infrastructure and the tight constraints on their resources, governments have increasingly sought to tap private sources of finance. Although most investment in infrastructure is still public, the private sector has increased in importance as governments have gained experience in regulating it.

These public-private partnerships can help a government stretch its budget further. They also spare the public sector the burden of running projects. But if the partnerships are to work, governments must be prepared to bear other responsibilities instead. They must establish autonomous regulatory agencies to oversee the activities of the private agents. The terms of the partnership must be written and monitored carefully, so that the private investor can earn an honest return but not a monopoly profit. It is also important for commercial risks to be borne by the private party. In too many cases, the division of labor has put profits in private hands, and risks in the public lap. There is now a great deal of accumulated, international experience with these partnerships. Some have been extremely successful in a wide variety of infrastructure areas, including telecommunications, roads, power generation, port management. But there have been equally numerous failures. Lessons should be drawn from both.

Governments must also resist the temptation to see infrastructure as a source of revenue. In telecommunications, for example, governments often allow private monopolies or quasi-monopolies to earn excessive profits, which the government can then tax to fill its coffers. This transfer from the consumer to the government, via the telecommunications giant, results in overpriced services, out of reach to large parts of the population. It may seem like a second-best solution for a cash-strapped government. But the damage to growth is likely to outweigh any fiscal benefits.

In short, governments should recognize that their own infrastructure investments are an indispensable complement to private efforts. If they abrogate the public investment function, it will not be replaced by private providers. Growth and delivery of basic services to the public will suffer as a result.

Human capital[14]

Investments in the health, knowledge, and skills of the people—human capital—are as important as investments in the more visible, physical capital of the country. Few economists would dissent from that statement. But they find it surprisingly hard to prove it statistically.

This is partly a problem of measurement. Empirical exercises usually try to find a connection between, say, education spending and growth. But spending on education should not be confused with the ultimate objective of education, which is to impart knowledge, the ability to learn, and noncognitive skills such as curiosity, empathy, and sociability. The same financial outlay can yield very different amounts of learning.

But even if researchers had better measures of education, they may have the wrong model of growth. Education may influence the economy in subtle ways, interacting with other factors. For example, India turned out world-class engineers and scientists for decades before its economy took off. This investment in skills yielded limited economic results until India discovered a global demand for software services (a demand which has since broadened to include outsourced research-and-development and a wide array of services delivered over the Internet). India, in short, had to solve a demand and supply problem, not just a supply problem.

Investments in human capital will generate opportunities for growth, including opportunities unforeseen at the time of the investment. But as India's experience demonstrates, those investments do not translate mechanically into growth. Other factors can intervene.

Education

Every country that sustained high growth for long periods put substantial effort into schooling its citizens and deepening its human capital. Conversely, considerable evidence suggests that other developing countries are not doing enough.

Education makes a legitimate claim on public money for at least two reasons. First, the Commission believes the social return probably exceeds the private return. (The research literature is full of controversy and disagreement on this point—debates that were aired during the Commission's workshops.) In other words, educated people contribute more to society

---

14 The Commission invited papers and held workshops on health, education, and growth. This section draws on those papers and discussions. There is, of course, a vast amount of research underway. As governments and donors focus attention and resources on health and education, the body of relevant experience is also growing quickly.

than they get back in higher pay, although the social return is notoriously difficult to measure.

Second, some families are credit-constrained and cannot borrow as much as they would like to spend on schooling, even if the higher wages a diploma or degree would fetch could more than repay the loan. Thus public spending on education is justified on the grounds of efficiency and equality of opportunity. It corrects the failure of the market to allocate enough resources to education, and it also widens access to education beyond those who can pay for it upfront.

The timing of education spending matters as well as the amount. Investments in early childhood raise the returns to investments later in life—children must learn how to learn. If they do not, they may never regain the lost ground, leaving a society sapped of potential and scarred by inequality.

How, then, should governments divide their budgets among primary, secondary, and tertiary education (that is, universities, colleges, and the like)? Developing countries, including the high-growth cases, have answered this question in a variety of ways. This suggests policy makers need not worry unduly about fine-tuning the mix in any precise way, provided they do not tilt it to one extreme or the other.

It seems reasonable to us to focus first on preschool and early childhood education, then on elementary education and literacy, and then increase the numbers in secondary school. Nor should governments forget the importance of a small tertiary sector that should grow as incomes rise and the demand for human capital sharpens. It is mostly from the tertiary sector, after all, that the government and private sector will fill its more senior, managerial ranks.

Researchers in this field have settled on "years of schooling" as a convenient, summary indicator of education. This is the measure they most often cite in debate, and it is much envied by their counterparts in health policy, who lack a single, "vulgar" measure (to use their term) in their field.

But years of schooling is only an input to education. The output—knowledge, cognitive abilities, and probably also social skills and other noncognitive skills—is often not captured. When it is measured, the results are often quite worrying. International tests in OECD countries, and also some developing countries, show that secondary school students vary enormously in what they actually learn (see figure 5).

Why do results vary so much? It is much too early to venture a strong opinion. We know that family background matters a lot, especially the parents' level of education and interest in schooling. In addition to demanding parents, demand from the market matters. When growth accelerates and demand for skills expands, the higher return to education strengthens incentives for schooling.

On the supply side, a combination of national exams and school autonomy works best, according to some experts. The ministry of education

Figure 5 PISA Results

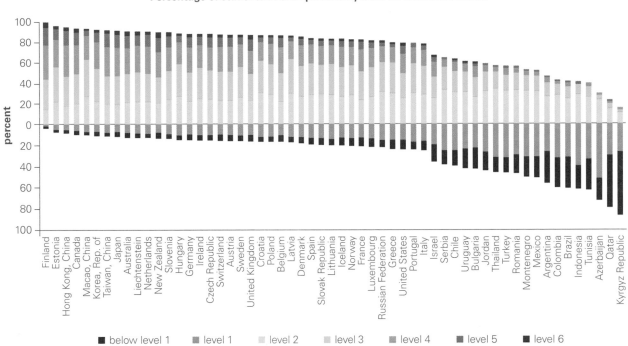

Percentage of students at each proficiency level on the science scale

Legend: ■ below level 1 ■ level 1 ■ level 2 ■ level 3 ■ level 4 ■ level 5 ■ level 6

Source: OECD PISA 2006 database, Table 2.1a. StatLink http://dc.dod.org/10.1787/141844475532.

Note: Countries are ranked in descending order of percentage of 15-year-old at Levels 2, 3, 4, 5, and 6.
Above the zero line one finds the proportion of students in the country that has higher ratings than level 1.
Below the zero line, one finds the proportion of students with level 1 and below.

should set centralized exams, but leave schools relatively free to decide how to meet those national tests. In particular, schools should enjoy autonomy in deciding their teachers' salaries and training.

Such a combination may explain Finland's success, relative to other OECD countries. But in poorer countries the reasons for success and failure may be less subtle. Some countries, for example, face a simple shortage of qualified teachers. The schooling budget may not be big enough to attract highly educated people, who enjoy more lucrative options in the private sector.

Moreover, once hired, teachers do not always face strong incentives to do a good job—or even to show up in class. In some countries, teaching positions are handed out as a form of political patronage. If people owe their jobs to a political favor, they are unlikely to do it well.

This is a knotty problem to solve, and some families decide they cannot afford to wait. Even those in poor households send their children to private schools, at the elementary and secondary levels, despite the financial sacrifice this entails. We have been surprised to learn how widespread private education has become in many developing countries, even among the poorest parts of the population. Most iniquitous are systems in which elite universities, financed from the public purse, set demanding entrance standards, which can be met only if people are wealthy enough to pay for high-quality private schooling.

We still need to know much more about education—how to get the most out of the government's budget, and how to get the best out of teachers and their students. We recommend this as a high priority for policy research. One place to start is measurement. The abilities of students—their literacy and numeracy—need to be gauged far more widely around the world. In other areas of government and business, measuring things and disclosing the results are known to change outcomes even without further intervention.

More research would help. But on the basis of the evidence we have already seen, it is hard to resist the conclusion that educational spending in many countries is marred by waste and inefficiency, even as the return to human capital is rising around the world. This inefficiency is a constraint on growth and a threat to equality of opportunity.

Health

Health is justifiably viewed by many as a right. It is an end in itself, which is deeply valued whether or not it also contributes to economic goals. The fact remains, however, that health does also affect economic performance in multiple ways.

For example, the threat of disease can deter investment in human capital. If households fear their children will not survive infancy, they are likely to have more offspring. But with lots of children to care for, they may not invest in educating each one.

Researchers are refining their estimates of these effects. Take malaria, for example. Where the disease is endemic, workers can expect to suffer two bouts of fever each year, losing 5–10 working days each time. That is a substantial loss of labor supply. Much worse is the damage childhood malaria may do to the cognitive development of infants.[15]

But one area stands out as critical. Indeed, ill health and poor nutrition in early childhood seems to have a first-order impact on both growth and equality. It does so by causing lasting harm to a child's ability to acquire cognitive and noncognitive skills as he or she moves up through school—harm that is impossible or very difficult to reverse. In a world where cognitive skills are rising in value, this damage will jeopardize equality of opportunity, and, if widespread, impair a country's economic potential far into the future.

It is not easy, however, to make this insidious problem a pressing political issue. The payoffs to interventions in early childhood emerge only in the

---

15 See Bloom, David, and Canning, David. 2008. "Population Health and Economic Growth." Background Paper, Commission on Growth and Development.

very long run. Moreover, children do not have a voice of their own, and cannot show their discontent with policy.

The recent run-up in food prices has highlighted the vulnerability of low-income groups to undernutrition. The potential consequences on their children may be severe. Prompt action to protect poorer groups is urgently needed; otherwise malnutrition will cause suffering and also reduce long-term growth prospects in a manner that is deeply unfair. The world does have the resources to deal with this problem, to which later parts of this report return.

Technology Transfer

In all the cases of sustained, high growth, the economies have rapidly absorbed knowhow, technology, and, more generally, knowledge from the rest of the world. These economies did not have to originate much of this knowledge, but they did have to assimilate it at a tremendous pace. That we know. What we do not know—at least not as well as we would like—is precisely how they did it, and how policy makers can hurry the process along. This is an obvious priority for research. As highlighted at the beginning of this report, economies can learn faster than they can invent. Knowledge acquired from the global economy is thus the fundamental basis of economic catch-up and sustained growth.

"Knowledge," in the language of economics, refers to any trick, technique, or insight that allows an economy to generate more out of its existing resources of land, labor, and capital. It includes the codified knowledge that can be set out in books, blueprints, and manuals, but also the tacit knowhow acquired through experience. The concept is a broad one, as Paul Romer, a member of the Commission's working group, has emphasized. It extends from abstract ideas, such as scientific formulae, to eminently practical ones, such as the traffic circle or roundabout.

Knowledge does not only consist of ideas for making more things, cheaper things, or new things. It includes the accumulated wisdom of human and social experience—as historians and social scientists interpret and reinterpret it. For example, the "invention" of the separation of powers between three branches of government, and the checks and balances it ensures, is possibly one of the most creative and influential innovations of the last few centuries. Many other institutional innovations have been tried and refined through trial and error, and have helped achieve economic and social goals more efficiently and fairly.

To economists, these ideas all share one characteristic: they are "nonrival." If you use or "consume" an idea, it does not stop me from also using it. Thomas Jefferson made a famous analogy with the light of a candle: If you light your candle with mine, it does not darken my flame.

"In this globalized world, physical capital and technology are always available. But human capital is still very immobile, so you should have good education and job-training programs to acquaint people with the necessary technology. Then capital and technology can be easily transferred to the developing economies to jump-start growth."

—Han Duck-soo

The value of knowledge in the global economy is high and rising. Indeed, the progress of the advanced economies depends mainly on innovation and new ideas. Technology also spreads more quickly now from the countries where it is invented to other parts of the world. For example, it took over 90 years after its invention for the telegram to spread to 80 percent of developing countries. It took only 16 years for the mobile phone to do so.[16]

What can developing economies do to ensure that they learn—to ensure that productive and institutional knowledge is transferred to the public and private sector?

One known channel is foreign direct investment (FDI). As well as money, FDI can bring a familiarity with foreign production techniques, overseas markets, and international supply chains. This expertise may be worth more than the capital itself. (China, which has recently experienced an excess of saving over investment, would probably prefer FDI without the "I"—although China is admittedly a unique case.) In developing countries, FDI is a small fraction of total investment. But because of the knowledge transfer it normally carries with it, its importance is much larger than its fractional contribution to total investment.

Foreign investors find it hard to keep their knowledge and expertise entirely to themselves. A multinational may train a local recruit, who later leaves to join another firm. It may share technology with a supplier, who then serves rival customers. Because know-how leaks beyond the borders of the firm into the wider economy, there is a natural tendency for the social return to FDI to exceed the private return. This creates some justification for government policies to encourage it.

Such policies fall into two categories: measures to attract more FDI, and measures to extract more knowledge from a given amount of investment. A common example of the first is a simple information campaign designed to introduce a country's investment opportunities to potential foreign investors. These can make a difference if foreign investors imperfectly perceive the opportunities and the risks of a potential location. They can also help if potential investors are all waiting for each other to be the "pioneer," who incurs the costs of finding out about a country.

Examples of the second type of policy—those that glean more knowledge from FDI—include obligations on the foreign investor to hire and train local staff as managers, even letting them advance to positions beyond their home country. A common organizational form for doing this is the joint venture. However, if such provisions are too onerous ("involuntary technology transfer" is the commonly used term), they will deter investors, especially those with valuable proprietary knowledge to lose. FDI occurs in a highly competitive international environment, and countries need to keep

---

16 World Bank. 2008. *Global Economic Prospects 2008: Technology Diffusion in the Developing World*. Washington, DC: World Bank.

the demands they put on foreign investors in balance with the alternatives offered by other potential hosts competing for the same knowledge and investment.

Whereas in most countries FDI is a relatively small fraction of total investment, in some cases, a single foreign investor looms large. This is more likely in small states where economic activity is concentrated in a few industries, such as mining or plantation agriculture. In these cases, care must be taken to prevent the foreign investor from exercising undue political influence. Excessive clout can undermine domestic governance, destroy trust, and sometimes opens the door to large-scale corruption.

Foreign education, particularly higher education, has proved to be an important channel of knowledge transfer. One of the first actions Japan took during the Meiji Restoration was to bring experts from the United States and Europe, and to send Japanese students to Western universities. A more recent and well-known example is China when it started reforms. At the invitation of leaders and officials from the Chinese government, a stream of foreign experts started to visit the country to help them learn about the workings of a market economy, the institutions underpinning it, and its responses to change. At the same time, a stream of Chinese students left to be trained in U.S. and European universities.

In general, higher education in advanced countries has figured prominently in the training of senior managers, policy makers, and political leaders in a wide range of countries. The results in terms of growth vary considerably. Notwithstanding ambiguous results, foreign education, ideally subsidized by advanced countries, is an underused channel for knowledge transfer in many countries. By studying abroad, students acquire international contacts, which will help them remain abreast of new thinking long after they have left the classroom.

Governments should expand such placements and international donors should fund them. Furthermore, these opportunities should not be limited to scientists and engineers, but should also include young people who are likely to serve in policy making and the civil service. We recommend that donors, including the international financial institutions, support a program of international exchanges for civil servants, so that government personnel from one developing country can visit and learn from their counterparts in another. Such programs now exist in some countries, particularly in Africa. Developing countries would gain if these programs were expanded, made more systematic, and extended beyond Africa.

"Technology comes with trade. So trade plays a very multidimensional role."

—*Han Duck-soo*

Competition and Structural Change

As it expands, an economy changes its shape and composition as well as its size. New industries emerge, older ones eventually fade. The growth

> *"Being exposed to competition brings out the best in institutions. A famous economist once said that the best of all monopoly profits is a quiet life. You don't want a quiet life for a firm; you want it forever trying to improve its productivity."*
>
> —*Robert Solow*

of GDP may be measured up in the macroeconomic treetops, but all the action is in the microeconomic undergrowth, where new limbs sprout, and deadwood is cleared away. From an economic point of view, this process is natural. As workers become better educated, better equipped, and better paid, some industries become newly viable; others cease to be so.

Joseph Schumpeter described this process as "creative destruction." Governments can hasten the process by encouraging the entry of new firms and the emergence of new industries. But what perhaps matters more is that they do not resist it.

They will certainly be called upon to do so. Some companies, for example, will argue they should be sheltered so that they can attain a big enough size to be efficient. The case is thought to be more compelling the smaller the economy. But it is a static argument. It dwells on the unit costs of big firms compared with small ones in an otherwise unchanging world. While incumbent firms press this case with the government, new companies or technologies may be waiting in the wings that will overturn the industry's cost structure or supplant the industry altogether. The static analysis, so commonly deployed, is simply misleading and a poor approach to productivity gains and growth.

In fact, some empirical studies suggest that economies owe most of their progress to the entry of new, more productive firms, and the exit of ailing ones. Improvements in the efficiency of incumbent firms play a smaller role. The dynamic productivity gains from entry and exit can overwhelm the static efficiency gains from scale. This means that entry and the threat of entry are important to ensure competition.

Just as the entry and exit of firms invigorates industries, so the rise and fall of industries breathes life into whole economies. Structural change under competitive pressure is what propels productivity growth. It is counterproductive to cling to stagnating industries, even industries that were once responsible for the country's growth. One of the most common mistakes, we have learned from a range of experiences, is to find a successful constellation of policies and industries, then stay with them for too long. When it comes to growth, very little if anything is permanent.

While creative destruction is economically natural, it doesn't feel natural to those displaced in the process. If these casualties of growth are simply disregarded, they will seek ways to slow the economy's progress. In intervening on their behalf, governments should be guided by two principles. First, they should try, as far as possible, to protect people, not jobs. Unemployment insurance, retraining, and uninterrupted access to health care are all ways to cushion the blows of the market, without shutting it down.

Second, if governments cannot provide much social protection, they may have to tread more carefully with their economic reforms. The speed of job destruction should not outstrip the pace of job creation.

Labor Markets

In poor, populous countries, labor is in surplus supply. Jobs are hard to come by, wages are low, and many people are self-employed out of necessity. This unhappy situation is what 7 percent growth sustained for decades is supposed to solve.

The solution starts by creating gainful employment, often in export industries, for people otherwise underemployed in the traditional or informal sectors. In the next stage, the economy creates better jobs, worthy of better educated, more skilful workers. For these stages to unfold, labor must be mobile. It must move from field to factory, and from one industry to another.

Perhaps the greatest analyst of a labor-surplus economy was Sir Arthur Lewis. In his models, the fields were so overmanned that the "marginal product" of agricultural labor was close to zero. In other words, if one field hand left the farm to work in an export factory, the farm would lose nothing. By the same token, if the worker were to add even one cent to the economy in his or her new factory job, society would gain.

The problem is that an export factory cannot tempt workers from the fields for one cent. They have to pay more than this. Therefore, the cost to the factory of hiring workers from the fields is greater than the opportunity cost of their labor. As a result, the social return to factory employment can be higher than the private return for a period of time. This period persists until the surplus labor is absorbed and the wages in the export sector converge to the opportunity cost in the traditional sector. This is one justification for the industrial policies, including the exchange rate policies, described in a subsequent section. They make investment in the export sector more profitable, bringing the private returns more into line with the social benefits.

There is much governments can do to increase labor mobility. For example, workers find it easier to pick up new skills and enter new trades if they are literate and educated. In addition, they will leave the countryside more readily if the cities are prepared to accommodate them. In a later section, we will discuss what governments can do to ease the strains of urbanization.

Beyond these outlays, governments can also try to overhaul labor market institutions and regulations. These institutions are complicated and various. Unsurprisingly, researchers disagree about how to reform them.

Some rules and institutions exist to safeguard the rights of labor, defending workers against exploitation, abuse, underage employment, and unsafe working conditions. In some countries, these rights are protected by unions or government regulations. But in others, no such protections are in place. The Commission feels strongly that these rights should not be sacrificed to achieve other economic objectives, including growth. Besides, labor viola-

"There's no doubt that sustained growth needs well-functioning labor markets. Today, we all know that the right approach is not to protect jobs in existing industries, but to protect employment by giving people the chance to get training and retraining. This kind of mobility is absolutely essential."

—Danuta Hübner

tions can have a commercial cost, thanks to growing international scrutiny of employment conditions and the threat of consumer boycotts.

In many economies, a formal labor market coexists with an informal one. Formal jobs typically offer better wages and terms than informal jobs, even if the jobholder is no better qualified. They can do so because they are fenced off by regulations or unions' agreement or a combination of the two, which prevents the vast pool of "outsiders" bidding down the wages of the "insiders." It is understandable that workers in the formal sector will fight to defend their privileges and resist competition from outside. In a surplus-labor economy, they are playing something close to a zero-sum game: there are only so many well-paid, tightly regulated jobs to go round. If you gain, I lose.

If demand for labor is strong enough, high costs and heavy regulations in the formal sector pose few problems. Firms that are enthusiastically hiring workers may not worry about restrictions on firing. Likewise, if the labor market is tight enough, the going wage rate will exceed any minimum wages stipulated by law. Many supposed regulatory impediments to growth decline in significance or vanish altogether in the face of excess demand for labor.

It is also not uncommon in policy debates in developing countries to hear that the problem is on the supply side: it is a matter of weaknesses in the labor force, not the weakness of labor demand. The underemployed population lack skills, the argument goes, therefore the solution is to train them. The aim is to upgrade labor supply, rather than stimulating labor demand.

There is a certain theoretical sense in which this argument is true. In principle, if workers were sufficiently educated and heavily trained, they would be worth the cost of hiring them, even with the full panoply of benefits and wages that prevail in the formal sector. But it is difficult, not to say extremely expensive, to upgrade the skills of workers before finding employment for them, partly because workers learn so much on the job. Thus, while there is no disagreement about the need for education and human capital investment, as a matter of strategy in many countries, this supply-side approach will often not be sufficient.

In most cases, the high cost of labor in the formal sector will deter investment, especially in export industries that must compete in the global marketplace. But any attempt to breach the divide between the formal and informal sectors will meet insurmountable resistance. How, then, can a country resolve this conundrum? What policies will simultaneously create jobs for the underemployed poor, permit a viable return to industry, and mollify the influential minority of workers already employed in the formal sector?

A pragmatic compromise is one possibility. Rather than imposing the full costs of the formal sector on employers, or inflicting unbridled wage competition on workers, governments could create an alternative employment track. They should allow export-oriented industries to recruit workers on easier terms than those that prevail in the formal sector. The government could, for example, create special economic zones with less onerous employment obligations. The virtue of this approach is that it creates room for employment to grow without threatening participants in the formal sector. The aim is to turn something close to a zero-sum game into a positive-sum one.

It should be emphasized that this alternative employment track would not be free of regulation. It would not be exempt from rules on health, safety, working hours, environmental conditions, and child labor. These rights are not negotiable.

Nonetheless, this approach to the labor market will not appeal to some. It will seem to exacerbate, rather than solve, the existing problem of "dualism," whereby the labor market is split into segments, each governed by different rules and different prices. In a way these charges are true. But the alternative is worse. It is to leave large fractions of the population blocked from higher productivity employment, consigned to breaking bricks or opening doors, rather than assembling toys or stitching garments.

The compromise suggested here should be a temporary one. If successful, wages and benefits in the new industries will eventually catch up with those in the formal sector. As the labor surplus declines, special provisions in the export zones can be removed. This is often exactly what happened in countries that have tried this approach. The country case studies contributed to the Commission show that special labor provisions and export zones were phased out over time as the need for them declined, and the distortions they created in employment, investment, and wages became more worrisome.

Even if they back this temporary compromise, governments should continue their efforts to reform the formal labor market. An overhaul would certainly be desirable. In India, for example, labor contracts that permit seasonal work in cyclical industries are problematic even though arguably in the interest of all parties. Our conclusion, born of experience, is merely that such reforms are politically difficult. Although worthwhile, they do not solve the underlying problem of the misalignment of the formal and informal sector. Therefore governments should not wait to win these battles before exploring other ways to jump-start job growth and export diversification.[17]

It is worth noting that China did not face quite the same problem. At the time of its reforms in 1978, there was no formal sector, just the state-owned sector, which spanned most of the industrial economy. The new enterprises and joint ventures in the export zones were no immediate threat to work-

---

17 The alternative employment framework for informal jobs may also be useful for things like part-time work, which would allow greater female labor force participation.

ers in the state-owned enterprises. And the government did not require the emerging export sector to offer the same wages or terms of employment as the state companies. Thus the exporters had direct access to the surplus labor in China's vast agricultural sector.

Getting the labor market right is vital to both the economics and politics of growth. In too many developing countries, a portion of the population has not enjoyed the benefits of economic advance, and does not anticipate enjoying them in the future. If they are forever blocked from employment, the economy will miss out on their labor and any growth strategy will lose their support.

Export Promotion and Industrial Policy

All of the sustained, high-growth cases prospered by serving global markets. The crucial role of exports in their success is not much disputed. But the role of export promotion is. Many of them tried a variety of policies to encourage investment in the export sectors in the early stages of their development, and several of these measures would qualify as industrial policies. They tried to promote specific industries or sectors through tax breaks, direct subsidies, import tariff exemptions, cheap credit, dedicated infrastructure, or the bundling of all of these in export zones.

Nonetheless, the significance of these policies is hard to prove. Even though most of the high-growth successful economies tried industrial policies, so did a lot of failures. Nor do we know the counterfactual: whether the high-growth cases would have succeeded even without targeted incentives.

All sides of this debate were reflected in the Commission's workshop on industrial policies, and in its own deliberations. The cut-and-thrust of the argument usefully clarified some of the virtues and risks of export promotion.

Some in the broader debate argue that industrial policies are not necessary. The private sector, in pursuit of profit, will discover where a country's comparative advantage lies and invest accordingly. Others argue that markets fall short in certain respects. Outside industrial investors (entering via FDI) may not know how to do business in a new location, for example. Those that enter first, regardless of whether they are successful, provide a benefit to other potential entrants. Their rivals and successors will learn from their experiment, without having borne the costs or risks. This can lead to a suboptimal level of experimentation, unless the government steps in to encourage it.

To take another example, in countries where large numbers of workers are underemployed in agriculture, the social return to factory employment may exceed the private return. It may be necessary to subsidize employment or investment outside agriculture to compensate for this gap. (This point is explained in greater detail in the section on labor markets.)

Some skeptics might concede that markets do not always work, but they argue that industrial policies don't either. This is either because governments do not know what they are doing—they lack the expertise to identify successful targets for investment, and will waste resources on plausible failures—or because they knowingly subvert the process to their own ends, dispensing favors to their industrial allies. There is, of course, considerable variation across countries in the competence of government and in the undue influence of special interests. But those who worry about government competence or capture would prefer to rule out promotional activities altogether. The risk of failure or subversion is too great, they say; better not to try.

But there are also risks to doing nothing. A flourishing export sector is a critical ingredient of high growth, especially in the early stages. If an economy is failing to diversify its exports and failing to generate productive jobs in new industries, governments do look for ways to try to jump-start the process, and they should.

These efforts should bow to certain disciplines, however. First, they should be temporary, because the problems they are designed to overcome are not permanent. Second, they should be evaluated critically and abandoned quickly if they are not producing the desired results. Subsidies may be justified if an export industry cannot get started without them. But if it cannot *keep* going without them, the original policy was a mistake and the subsidies should be abandoned. Third, although such policies will discriminate in favor of exports, they should remain as neutral as possible about which exports. As far as possible, they should be agnostic about particular industries, leaving the remainder of the choice to private investors.[18] Finally and importantly, export promotion is not a good substitute for other key supportive ingredients: education, infrastructure, responsive regulation, and the like.

Exchange Rates

In the developing world, most governments and central banks feel they cannot afford to take their eye off the foreign value of their currency. But efforts to shepherd exchange rates are as controversial as industrial policies. Indeed, they can be thought of as a form of industrial policy. If a government resists an appreciation of the currency, or if it devalues, it is, in effect,

---

18 This last is not a rigid rule. For example, training for particular industries may be warranted, especially if private companies underinvest in transferable skills, because they fear that workers will carry those skills with them to a rival firm. But these types of sector-specific support work best when they follow rather than lead private investment.

imposing an across-the-board tax on imports and providing a subsidy to exports.

Economists have lined up equally passionately for and against such policies. Max Corden describes them as a kind of protectionism. Others, such as Bela Balassa, thought they held the key to development. This is how John Williamson, a fellow at the Peterson Institute for International Economics, has described Balassa's position: "give [a country] an exchange rate sufficiently competitive that its entrepreneurs are motivated to go and sell on the world market, and it will grow. Give it too much easy money from oil exports, or aid, or capital inflows, and let its exchange rate appreciate in consequence, and too many people with ability will be diverted from exporting to squabbling about the rents, and growth will be doomed."[19]

Many of the countries that enjoyed sustained, high growth have shared Balassa's exchange rate convictions at various times. To keep the currency competitive, they have regulated the amount and type of capital flowing across their borders. They have also accumulated foreign reserves in the central bank. A mixture of the two policies was normal.

The use of exchange rates for "industrial policy," that is to maintain export competitiveness, has the advantage of being neutral between industrial sectors. It does not make big demands on government discretion and expertise. However, it has its own costs and risks.

For one thing, these policies can limit the amount of capital a country imports from overseas. This raises the cost of capital, which will tend to reduce investment. Indeed, these policies create an interesting trade-off. They make investment in the export sector more appealing. But they simultaneously make capital less readily available.[20]

Second, management of the exchange rate is sometimes used as a substitute for productivity-enhancing investments in education and human capital or for other crucial elements of a growth strategy, such as inbound knowledge transfer. When used in this way, it results in growth, purchased at the price of very low wages commensurate with equally low productivity levels.

Third, where surplus labor is no longer available, or labor unions are strong, an undervalued exchange rate may lead to higher pay demands and a wage-price spiral that is detrimental to sustained growth prospects.

At best, management of the exchange rate can be used for two purposes. One is to tip the balance slightly in favor of exports in the early stages of growth, to overcome informational asymmetries and other potential transitory frictions. The other is to prevent a surge of capital inflows (which may be transitory) from disrupting the profitability and growth of the export sectors.

"Fixed exchange rates can lead to all kinds of imbalances, pent-up problems and ultimately duress and even crisis, as happened in the 1990s. So I think it is very much in the interest of each developing country to move toward a flexible exchange rate. Obviously if you have a relatively fixed rate to begin with, you've got to find some way to do that at a pace that enables the rest of your financial and economic system to adjust to the change."

—Robert Rubin

---

19 Williamson, John. 2003. Review of "Too Sensational" by Max Corden. *Journal of Economic Literature* 41(4): 1289–90.

20 Williamson, John. 2003. "Exchange Rate Policy and Development." Initiative for Policy Dialogue.

If pursued to extremes, holding the exchange rate down will result in a big trade surplus. This is not in the country's own interest, as it involves forsaking current consumption in order to lend to foreigners. Nor will surpluses go down well with the neighbors. By keeping its currency cheap, a country makes its trading partners' currencies more expensive. When a large country like China does this, it does not escape notice. Trade partners, who feel China's exporters enjoy an unfair advantage, may threaten to retaliate with tariffs. That is in no one's interest.

Is "export promotion" a polite term for crude mercantilism? In the 18th century, some European powers thought the goal of economic statecraft was simply to sell more to foreigners than you bought from them, resulting in a trade surplus and an inflow of gold bullion.

The case of high-growth economies is different. To catch up with the advanced economies, countries will need to increase the size of their export sector, so that exports as a percentage of GDP will increase. But that is only one side of the ledger. On the other side, imports can and should also increase. The goal of an export-led strategy is not to increase reserves or to run a trade surplus. It is to increase exports to enable incremental productive employment, larger imports, and ultimately faster growth. (See also our discussion of the "adding-up" problem in part 4.)

The more a country earns from its exports, the more it can afford to benefit from imports, especially the equipment and machinery that embody new technologies. If, on the other hand, exports flag, the shortage of foreign exchange will limit what a country can buy-in from abroad and hamper its progress.

As with other forms of export promotion, exchange rate policies can outlive their usefulness. If the currency is suppressed by too much or for too long, it will distort the evolution of the economy by removing the natural market pressure for change. The cheap currency will tend to lock activity into labor-intensive export sectors, reduce the return to upgrading skills, and eventually harm productivity as a result. Like other industrial policies, a keenly priced currency is supposed to solve a specific, transitory problem. Eventually, as an economy grows more prosperous, domestic demand should and usually does play an increasingly important role in generating and sustaining growth. Exchange rate policy should not stand in the way of this natural evolution.

"The East Asian experience since the 1960s—the tigers, the dragons, and now China, Vietnam, and others—demonstrates the role of a competitive exchange rate in rapid growth. In all cases, this was achieved through a combination of restrictions on capital inflows and monetization of inflows."

—*Zhou Xiaochuan*

Capital Flows and Financial Market Openness

Economists would readily agree that financial openness is beneficial in the long run. No one now advocates capital controls for America or the European Union. But analysts will also confess to considerable uncertainty and some disagreement about the timing and sequencing of moves to open up.

None of the sustained, high-growth cases that we know about were particularly quick to open their capital accounts. Yet developing countries have come under considerable pressure from international financial institutions and economic commentators, urging them to unlock the financial gates. Whether this is good advice seems to us to depend heavily on whether the economy is diversified, its capital markets mature, and its financial institutions strong.

Even if one thinks controls on capital inflows and outflows are desirable at certain stages of growth, are they feasible? Can they be effective? There are indeed many ways of circumventing capital controls, and financial markets have proven exceptionally creative in exploiting them. But policies that actively discourage speculative, short-term capital inflows have proven useful in turbulent times. The fact that controls may be leaky and imperfect does not seem a decisive argument against them. Many other policies—taxes, for example—are also leaky and imperfect. That is not a reason to abandon them altogether; merely a reason to implement them better.

Developing countries like to exercise some control over the exchange rate, both to maintain the competitiveness of their exports, and also to offset damaging bouts of exchange rate volatility. Capital controls allow a developing country to do this while also controlling inflation. Absent controls, large capital inflows give central bankers no choice but to let the currency strengthen or to accumulate reserves, a policy which implies a loss of monetary control. To put the same point slightly differently: every country wants and needs to control inflation. If it also wishes to exercise some independent control over the exchange rate (for competitive reasons or just to control volatility), then it needs capital controls.[21]

This is why many countries favor capital controls until such time as the structural transformation of the economy is well advanced. It is difficult to be precise as to when exactly the point of "well advanced" is reached. And the exact timing of when the controls should be lifted is a controversial matter. Some believe that middle-income countries, economically diversified, and with diversified and deep local financial markets and strong links to the world economy are better off with an inflation-targeting regime, allowing relatively free capital flows and flexible exchange rates ("dirty floats"). But to avoid damaging currency overvaluations, such economies would be well advised to maintain a strong fiscal position that would permit them to accumulate international reserves without loss of monetary control.

> "Keeping exchange rates competitive should be a principal objective of policy in emerging economies. Central banks should stand ready to buy up to the last dollar. The pressure on central banks can be relieved by placing controls on capital inflows. Yes, capital controls are leaky, but so are taxes, and that does not stop governments from trying to tax their citizens."
>
> —Pedro-Pablo Kuczynski

21 The proposition more precisely is that if a country has an open capital account and manages its exchange rate it will not be in control of the money supply. Thus, it is dependent on other instruments to manage inflationary pressures; fiscal policy being the obvious candidate. Fiscal policy is a very imperfect substitute for monetary policy in dealing with inflation.

Macroeconomic Stability

No economy can flourish in the midst of macroeconomic instability. Wild fluctuations in the price level, the exchange rate, the interest rate, or the tax burden serve as a major deterrent to private investment, the proximate driver of growth. Economists and policy makers, however, disagree about the precise definition of stability and the best way to preserve it.

For example, very high inflation is clearly damaging to investment and growth. Bringing inflation down is also very costly in terms of lost output and employment. But how high is very high? Some countries have grown for long periods with persistent inflation of 15–30 percent.[22] With central banks in Europe, the United States, and developing countries now targeting much lower rates, this threshold appears excessive. The consensus now is that inflation should be kept stable and in single digits. However, the benefits of bringing it to very low levels are unclear.

There is widespread agreement that central banks can best fight inflation if given a degree of autonomy from political imperatives. In particular, a central bank should be insulated from the potentially irresponsible behavior of politicians, who may want it to relax its grip on inflation before elections, or to bankroll their spending plans. As they have become more autonomous, central banks have become much better at controlling inflation all over the world, without harming growth.

At the same time, central banks have sometimes been criticized for appearing indifferent to the need of the real economy and unresponsive to political demands. In a mature market economy, the downsides of central bank independence seem pretty modest. The central bank's commitment to price stability does not greatly endanger any of the economy's other objectives. And if its commitment results in higher interest rates or a more volatile exchange rate, the private sector has the flexibility and the financial instruments to cope.

In a developing economy, the issue is more complicated. The desirable effects of independence do not go away. But the economy must also maintain a coherent economic strategy. High-speed growth relies on export growth and a rapid integration into the global economy. That process is affected by exchange rates, interest rates, and inflation. Thus the central bank's choices in all three areas bear heavily on the implementation of a growth strategy. Judgment is required to balance the benefits of autonomy and the need for coherence. In some countries this balance is achieved by having the Minister of Finance set the objectives and broad parameters of macroeconomic policies, and then leaving the Central Bank free to operate within these parameters.

---

22 Fischer, Stanley. 1993. "The Role of Macroeconomic Factors in Growth." *Journal of Monetary Economics* 32(3): 485–512.

Fiscal policy poses similar dilemmas. Rigid fiscal rules, which set ceilings for deficits, debt, current spending, and the like, help policy makers avoid costly mistakes. There are certainly times and places in which avoidance of mistakes is the first priority and rigid rules can be essential for this purpose. However, these rules can become counterproductive if applied too strictly for too long. In the words of one of the workshop participants, fiscal and monetary rules need to be left with an element of "creative ambiguity."

The concern is that the rules may be too rigid. They may set a fixed ceiling on fiscal deficits, for example. But deficits are more or less reckless depending on how quickly an economy is growing. If GDP is increasing quickly enough, then the government can run quite a big deficit without the ratio of debt to GDP ever growing. The ambiguities do not end there. Growth may itself depend on government investment, which may relieve infrastructure bottlenecks, for example. If the government cuts this investment to meet a fiscal deficit target, growth may falter, leaving the medium-run debt-to-GDP ratio no better off than before.

Thus, pragmatism suggests that any assessment of the public finances should take account of the economy's growth rate, and the effect of public expenditure on that growth.

Savings

Just as growth depends on investment, investment depends on a country's ability to finance it—out of its own savings or from foreign sources. There are limits to the latter, however, because foreign borrowing is risky. These limits are not very precise. But when they are breached the consequences can be very costly as many debt crises remind us. What is important to keep in mind is that there is no case of a sustained high investment path not backed up by high domestic savings. This raises the question, what drives savings? There is an old controversy which remains unresolved: do savings drive investment? Or do investments generate their own savings? Probably the causation runs in both directions. It depends on whether the economy has underutilized resources that can be transformed into investment, but the truth is that experts in this area have not yet come to firm conclusions.[23]

Savings have three components: household, corporate, and government.

Government saving is the percentage of its investment that is financed out of revenues (that percentage can exceed 100 when the government covers its investment and also pays back debt). The number can be less than zero if the government is financing its current expenditure, which can include redistribution programs, with debt. To sustain adequate levels of public investment,

---

23 Deaton, Angus. 1999. "Saving and Growth," in Luis Serven and Klaus Schmitt-Hebbel, *The Economics of Savings and Growth*. Cambridge, UK: Cambridge University Press.

government revenues need to be high enough to support current expenditures on service delivery and a part of the investment program.

But governments are often short of revenues, and wary of imprudent borrowing. As a result, public investment is commonly crowded out by demands for current expenditures and redistribution. This partly reflects a political process that places a higher value on current consumption relative to future consumption, which is both more distant in time and less certain to materialize.[24] For public sector investment to survive, government revenue needs to be adequate to the task.

The second element of savings is corporate. Companies retain profits, rather than distributing them to shareholders, and reinvest them in the business, wherever they think the return is likely to exceed the cost of capital. This component of saving, then, is largely driven by the returns to private investment.

Companies also turn to external financing to pay for investment projects. Start-up companies, for example, often have little in the way of retained earnings to finance new ventures. Some of this extra financing can come from abroad, as is the case with FDI. But experience suggests that most of it needs to come from domestic saving.

The determinants of household savings are complex and not fully understood. They are affected by income levels, demographics, the presence or absence of social insurance systems. There may also be cultural differences that show up in the propensity to save.

Household savings may be too low to finance high levels of private investment. One reason may be the lack of secure and accessible vehicles for saving. Many poor households lack a bank account. They store their wealth in jewelry, or by investing in their own tiny businesses. In neither case is the household's saving available to other, more productive firms to invest. This lack of saving vehicles could have a first-order negative impact on growth.

Conversely, another cause of high savings can be the lack of social insurance, pensions, and public funding of social services. In many countries, households, including poor ones, save for their own retirement, their children's education, and to insure themselves in the event of ill health. These choices represent socially very costly incentives for high savings. They should not be taken as having prescriptive value.

There are very few developing countries in which savings exceed investment by large amounts, with the notable exception of oil exporters and other resource-rich countries. China's excess savings, as measured by its

---

24 Government saving is a matter of collective but not individual choice, and hence is determined by somewhat different factors from those that affect household saving choices. There are a few cases of required (by law) individual or household savings. Singapore is one example. It does not seem to us that this model is likely to have wide applicability.

current account surplus, recently grew from modest levels (about 3 percent of GDP) to quite high (12 percent of GDP) in 2007. That is an unusual configuration, even for China, which has had a high rate of saving and investment since its 1978 reforms. Generally, running savings well above investment levels is a bad idea except for resource-rich countries, especially during times of booming resource prices. The deferred consumption would be better enjoyed in the present. And large countries that sustain high surpluses expose themselves to the charge of mercantilism.

Countries with large oil reserves often invest a large portion of their export earnings abroad. If their resource rents are very large, it normally doesn't make sense to consume or invest them domestically. But the scale of their overseas investments has aroused concern in some quarters. It is hard to know what other options oil-exporters have. If they were not permitted to invest their oil earnings abroad, their next best strategy would be to leave the oil in the ground. That would probably not be in anyone's interest.

Financial Sector Development

A well-developed financial system can help an economy grow by mobilizing savings, allocating funds to investment, and redistributing risk. But the pattern of financial sector maturation varies considerably among countries. Here we focus on a few key issues.

If the financial system fails to reach large portions of the population, household savings will be stunted. People need a secure, accessible vehicle for storing their wealth. If the banks do not provide it, people will save less, or store their money in less liquid forms that do not serve the wider economy well.

The absence of savings channels is inequitable as well as inefficient. The same can be said of the uneven provision of other types of financial services, including credit and secure transactions at reasonable cost. The burgeoning field of microfinance is addressing these issues with beneficial effects in many countries.

Deprived of savings accounts and bank loans, the poor also often lack secure title to their physical assets. Without property rights and the means to enforce them, they may struggle to obtain a loan from a formal financial institution. This reduces their access to credit, which makes it harder for them to start a business or expand one.

As the 2007–08 credit crunch demonstrates, even well-developed financial sectors are prone to shocks and crises. In emerging economies, financial crises can have devastating consequences for growth. Multiple banks can fail and whole swathes of industry can go bankrupt. Private liabilities quickly become public ones.

Financial crises can originate at home or overseas, and they can play out within a country's border or across them.

One common cause of internal crises is unsustainable public spending. Unable to raise the resources to pay its bills, a reckless government may order the central bank to print money instead. This will end in hyperinflation, unless the central bank has enough autonomy to refuse the government's demands.

Internal crises can also result from imprudent banks. In the early stages of development, the banking system provides most of the credit in an economy. (Bond markets emerge only later, as the capacity to issue, rate, and trade these securities develops.) Careful regulation and supervision are required to prevent banks from expanding credit too far.

The worst financial crises are often those that have an external dimension, involving foreign as well as domestic capital. Indeed, the threat of such conflagrations is one reason why countries impose capital controls. There are no precise guidelines for opening up to foreign capital and minimizing the risk of financial crises. But there is now a consensus that countries should open up, removing capital controls, only in step with their financial market maturity. Excessive speed introduces unnecessary risk and excessive slowness raises the cost of capital.

However, openness and maturity are linked. One way to speed up financial sector development is to invite foreign financial firms to invest in the sector. Just as FDI brings expertise to domestic industry, so the entry of foreign banks might raise the game of domestic ones, making them more robust. Governments will naturally want foreign banks to meet the same regulatory demands as domestic financial institutions. However, foreign banks may be reluctant to set up shop in a developing economy if they cannot conduct financial transactions fairly freely across borders. Again there are interesting trade-offs and dilemmas. The more open a financial system, the more mature it will become. But the more open a financial system, the more mature it needs to be. The quality of regulation has a direct bearing on the speed of safe capital market opening.

Urbanization and Rural Investment

This year, the world will pass an important threshold: half the world's people will live in cities. Over the next two decades, as the global population increases, most of that growth will take place in cities in the developing world (see figure 6).

People migrated from the countryside to the towns during Britain's industrial revolution, and they have done so in every industrial revolution since. It is extremely rare to achieve per capita incomes above $10,000

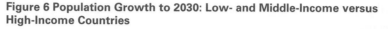

Figure 6 Population Growth to 2030: Low- and Middle-Income versus High-Income Countries

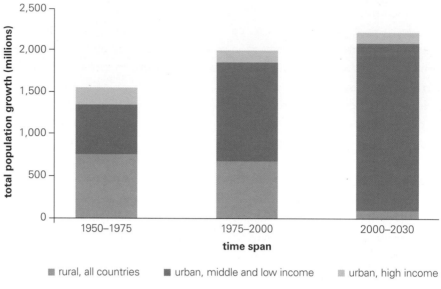

Source: United Nations Urbanization Prospects.

(in purchasing power parity terms) before half of the population lives in the cities. Urbanization is the geographical corollary of industrialization: as workers leave the farms for the factories, they leave the fields for the cities.

Although no country has industrialized without also urbanizing, in no country has this process been entirely smooth. Many fast-growing cities in the developing world are disfigured by squalor and bereft of public services. It is easy to conclude that urbanization is an unpleasant side effect of growth, best to be avoided. But this is a mistake. The proper response is not to resist urbanization, but to make it more orderly.

Cities thrive because of what economists call "agglomeration economies." When activities are clustered closely together, they can reap economies of scale and scope. Information also flows more efficiently. Valuable tricks of the trade seem to leak into the air, as Alfred Marshall, the great Victorian economist, observed.

But if cities thrive on scale and density, they also choke on congestion and pollution. In Cairo, the average daytime noise is 85 decibels, according to a report by Egypt's National Research Center.[25] That, *The New York Times* reports, is louder than a freight train 15 feet away.

To an economist, both the advantages of cities and their drawbacks represent "externalities" that are difficult to measure or price. (Your noise deafens me, but you do not compensate me for it. Likewise, I benefit from

---

25 Slackman, Michael. 2008. "A City Where You Can't Hear Yourself Scream." *The New York Times*, April 14.

copying your techniques or poaching your workers, but I do not compensate you for it.) That may be one reason why they are so hard to manage.

The traditional response to these externalities is planning and regulation. Zoning laws, for example, keep factories at a civilized distance from homes, where their noise, commotion, and pollution are less bothersome. But a delicate balance needs to be struck. Unrealistic regulations can fail or backfire. Some cannot be enforced. Others do bite, but make matters worse. If building codes are too strict, for example, cheap housing will be illegal. Nor should governments resort to planning regulations to mask what is really an underlying shortage of infrastructure. If water is not reaching every household in a dense urban area, the answer is to lay more water pipes, not to clear some households out.

Fast-growing cities need to extend infrastructure quickly. But city authorities cannot raise the money to build it at the pace required. The growth of economic activity in a city's limits often far outstrips the growth of its tax base. Therefore money will have to be provided by the central government. An alternative is to sell land or lease it. This has risks—public land can be sold too cheaply in transactions that are not arm's-length and at market prices—but the opportunity to raise large sums outweighs the dangers. In the absence of municipal financing mechanisms and an established tax base, land is one of the principal assets that can be sold and converted to needed infrastructure. Defining suitable guidelines and parameters would be a useful area of research.

As others have noted, the financial system can be as important to the growth of cities as cranes or earthmovers. Financial institutions make it possible for municipalities or private buyers to borrow the money for real estate purchases. As financial liberalization has spread, so too has housing finance. This is to be welcomed: mortgages allow property buyers to spread the cost of housing over longer periods, making it more affordable. But home lenders can be reckless, as recent events in America and Britain show. Mortgages are also the wrong answer if home building is constrained. In this case, mortgage finance will only increase the demand for a fixed supply of houses, resulting in pricier homes, not more homes.

As property prices rise in booming cities, so do the political demands for housing subsidies. Singapore used subsidized housing to narrow inequality and instill a sense of nationhood in its citizens. But it would be hard for other governments to emulate the experience of this city-state, which is small and unusually well administered. Rent subsidies distort private decisions. They also rapidly become very costly. Even America does not reach more than a fraction of eligible people with its rent subsidy.

Some people believe the problems of the cities can be solved out in the fields. Investment in rural areas might slow the tide of migrants to the cities, allowing for a more orderly urbanization.

"Ten or more years ago, the Chinese central government resisted urbanization, which the authorities thought was too rapid. This deserves to be on the list of 'bad ideas' because it ignores the importance of agglomeration efficiencies. The Chinese government has since reversed policy. It now understands the key role of urbanization in structural transformation. But urbanization poses a number of challenges. One is to develop an urban tax base and revenue system. Land rights are also extremely important: land is the most valuable asset in urban settings; how it is allocated determines how urbanization takes place. Another problem is how to subsidize housing efficiently. The pressure to subsidize housing through rent controls needs to be resisted."

—Zhou Xiaochuan

There are many good reasons to invest in agriculture. The rewards can be impressive. Agricultural research and extension yield returns of around 35 percent in Sub-Saharan Africa and 50 percent in Asia, according to the latest *World Development Report*. Moreover, in many developing countries, rural areas are where the bulk of the poor still live and work. To find jobs for this population in the urban economy will take several decades, even in the most dynamic economies. India, for example, is still about 70 percent rural. In China, which has been growing at 9–10 percent a year for almost 30 years, 55 percent of the population still lives in the countryside. Rural populations are often underserved by public services, which prompts some to seek better education or health care in the cities. The evidence also suggests that agricultural growth reduces poverty faster than growth in manufacturing or services.

Governments should invest in agriculture, then, insofar as such investments are justified on their own merits. But as a way to slow the growth of cities, rural investment is likely to disappoint. In many countries, especially in Africa, the growth of cities is mostly due to natural population increases and not migration. In addition, if rural investment raises the productivity of agriculture, it may simply reduce the demand for farm labor, adding to the pressure to leave the land.

If history is any guide, large-scale migration to the cities is part and parcel of the transformation economies must go through if they are to grow quickly. No country has ever caught up with the advanced economies through farming alone. In countries that in the last 50 years sustained episodes of 7 percent growth or more over 25 years or longer, manufacturing and services led the way (see figure 7). In a few cases agriculture actually shrank. Of course, prior gains in agricultural productivity may have freed up workers to fill the factories. But by the same token, the outmigration of surplus workers from agriculture will, at a certain point, allow land to be consolidated into larger plots. This should permit more capital-intensive and productive farming.

Ultimately a successful city will need urban planning, building codes, and robust property rights. It will need drainage, sewerage, rapid transit, and a sophisticated financial system capable of mobilizing the funds for these. But accumulating this infrastructure, expertise, and sophistication takes time. Governments should avail themselves of whatever shortcuts they can find, including the experience and expertise of other cities that have gone through this turmoil before them.

Equity and Equality of Opportunity

It is our belief that equity and equality of opportunity are essential ingredients of sustainable growth strategies. The evidence from both high and low

Figure 7 Growth Rates by Sector

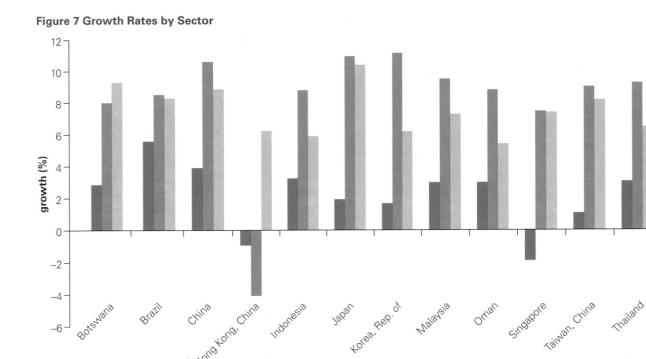

Source: See appendix, p. 114.

cases supports this view. The benefits of brisk growth are spread widely but not evenly. The rural poor do gain. But the experience of sustained growth in the modern era clearly suggests city-dwellers gain more—and to some extent this is inevitable. In the early stages of development, measured productivity in the cities is often 3–6 times that in the rural areas. As people move across this divide, measured inequality increases. This rise is not permanent, but it can take decades to run its course. The extent of inequality needs to be managed.

Albert Hirschman, the great development economist, compared this process to a two-lane traffic jam. If one lane begins to move, drivers in the other at first take comfort, inferring that their lane will also move soon. But the longer they remain stuck, the more frustrated they will become. The other lane becomes a provocation, not a consolation.[26]

The workshop on this topic made an important distinction between equity and equality of opportunity. The former concept refers to outcomes or results: people differ greatly in the incomes they earn, the health they enjoy, the security they possess, and so on. The latter idea, equality of opportunity, refers to starting points. It turns on such things as access to nutrition, education, and job opportunities.

---

26 Hirschman, Albert. 1981. "The Changing Tolerance for Income Inequality in the Course of Economic Development," in *Essays in Trespassing*. Cambridge, UK: Cambridge University Press.

"In many ways, the more equitable the growth, the more sustainable it's likely to be, because there will be less controversy, less disagreement, less resistance, and also there's an enormous amount of talent in populations that needs to be tapped. Excluding some parts of the population, whether by gender, age, or ethnicity, from the benefits of growth loses the talents that they have. So in my view, it is not only desirable that they go together, it's useful that they go together."

—Robert Solow

People care about both kinds of equality. But they understand that markets do not produce equal outcomes. They will tolerate this inequality, provided governments take steps to contain it. Generally, this means two things. One is making sure that income and essential services are extended to the poorer part of the population. The second, more controversial, is addressing the upper end of the income distribution, which in many cases exhibits vast accumulating wealth and appears to be living in a different, much richer country. Sharing this wealth through the tax system, and appropriate spending programs, including the funding of service provision and public sector investment, is an important part of social and political cohesion, and hence of the sustainability of the growth process. Judgment is required here. Carried to excess, redistribution can damage incentives and deter investment and risk taking.

Inequality of opportunity, on the other hand, does not involve trade-offs and can be toxic. This is especially so if opportunities are systematically denied to a group due to its ethnicity, religion, caste, or gender. Such injustices undermine social peace and spark political unrest. They will ultimately jeopardize buy-in and derail the economy's growth strategy.

The distribution of income in successful, high-growth economies varied a lot: Botswana had a Gini coefficient of 0.61 in 1993, Indonesia 0.34. But all showed a commitment to equality of opportunity. Failure on this score harms the economy directly, by leaving talents underexploited. It also distorts the pattern of investment. According to a paper for the Commission by Abhijit Banerjee of the Massachusetts Institute of Technology, the middle ranks and the poor underinvest in their businesses, because they are denied equal access to capital. The rich, on the other hand, invest too much.[27]

Inequality of opportunity also sows longer-term dangers. If one group is persistently and flagrantly excluded from the fruits of growth, the chances are they will eventually find a way to derail it. To extend Hirschman's metaphor, they will try to force their way into the other lane, disrupting traffic in both. Conversely, evidence from many countries suggests people will make great sacrifices for the sake of economic progress if they believe *their* children and grandchildren will enjoy a fair share of the rewards.

How can governments safeguard equality of opportunity and contain inequality of outcomes? The latter goal may be served by redistribution, over and above the informal sharing arrangements that often prevail in extended families and tight-knit communities. Equality of opportunity is best served by providing universal access to public services like health and education, and by meritocratic systems in government and the private sector.

---

27 Banerjee, Abhijit. 2007. "Investment Efficiency and the Distribution of Wealth." Background Paper, Commission on Growth and Development.

It is also served by building what might be called the infrastructure of popular capitalism. Titling programs, inspired by the work of the Peruvian economist Hernando de Soto, give poor people secure rights to their property. Microfinance and "mesofinance" allow small- and medium-scale entrepreneurs to invest more than they can save, loosening the knots identified by Banerjee. Over the past 15 years, donors, businesses, and social entrepreneurs have embraced these ideas and made considerable progress on the ground.

Some of the sharpest divisions fall within the household, where women lack the opportunities their male relatives enjoy. Some countries still struggle to get girls through school: almost one out of five girls who enroll does not complete primary school. They are encumbered by domestic chores or deterred by the lack of basic facilities like bathrooms. This denial of opportunity can be passed on to the next generation: women who lack a primary school education are less likely to send their children to school. Indeed, their children are only about half as likely to survive infancy.[28] It seems to us that the logical place to try to break this cycle is to focus on the obstacles (financial, safety, employment opportunities, sanitary facilities, and other) that prevent girls from completing the journey from school entry to productive employment. Young women play a pivotal role in education, health, and fertility rates; they are also potentially successful economic agents. Therefore enabling women to move successfully through education to productive employment will have a very high payoff in terms of long-term growth and poverty reduction.

Regional Development

Just as the impact of growth is felt unevenly across the population, so it falls unevenly across regions. Some states, provinces, and cities prosper rapidly, whereas others can lag behind. These spatial patterns can reflect the fundamentals of geography—a harbor or an ore deposit, for example—or the history of agglomeration: firms migrate to a location because others have moved there.

Governments can influence these forces, by deciding where to invest and build infrastructure, thus making the spatial distribution of opportunity more equal. But they should resist the temptation to counteract them, however politically demanding it can be at times. Regional policies should not try to produce uniformity across space in the pattern of growth and development.

"Unity, not uniformity" is a guiding principle of the European Union's regional development programs, which will amount to €347.4 billion over

"There is no contradiction between equality, redistribution and growth. Quite the contrary. Prosperity that is shared is not only morally right, it also gives people a chance to lift themselves out of poverty, creates legitimacy for responsible economic policies and can have an enhancing effect on long-term growth and prosperity."

—Carin Jämtin

---

28 UNICEF. *The State of the World's Children 2007: The Double Dividend of Gender Equality.*

the seven years to 2013. These programs try to reduce income and wealth gaps across countries and regions over time. As a result of recent enlargements, the most prosperous member of the union, Luxembourg, is now seven times richer than the poorest one, Romania. The EU's regional policies try to add to its "cohesion," which includes a sense of belonging to the union and owing obligations to it. It is ready to collaborate with developing countries to share experiences. China, Brazil, and India have already taken up this offer.

Firms base their location decisions on the provision of infrastructure, delivery of public services, and other public policies. A sound regional policy will invest in less developed areas to make them more competitive and thus more attractive to private investors.

If workers are also mobile, they can and do move away from depressed regions where labor is in excess supply. Thus, labor mobility is a partial substitute for regional policy. It is not a full substitute because some people, such as the elderly, will never be very mobile. And in many countries languages place a limit on mobility, as in the EU. Over time, the educational system should reduce these barriers to mobility. Nevertheless, the priority attached to regional investments should depend on the mobility of the people they are trying to help.

Such policies will also have a greater impact if they seek to improve labor mobility. In the EU, mobility is a long-term goal. Some obstacles, such as language barriers, are harder to remove than others. The EU is, for example, striving to ensure that credentials and licenses awarded in one member state are recognized in another.

Governments should try to make sure that workers move for the right reasons—in pursuit of a better job, for instance—but not the wrong ones—fleeing substandard education or health care, for example. The central government will need to invest in urban infrastructure, because emerging cities cannot raise money, either from taxes or borrowing, sufficient to the task. Investments in roads, rail, and telecommunications make it easier for labor to move, albeit in some respects less necessary. Indeed, many services can now be delivered at a distance, thanks to advances in communications technologies.

One important aspect of regional policy is fiscal. Developing countries raise the bulk of their taxes at the national level. Thus, the central government's fiscal powers dwarf those of state or local governments. And yet responsive government often requires a decentralized administration, in which decisions are taken close to home.

How, then, should the central government share its tax receipts with states, provinces, and municipalities? Countries vary enormously in how they divide revenues and responsibilities. In China, for example, the central government appoints governors and mayors, who are rotated from one province to another. Their performance is judged against objectives set by the central government. Compared with more formally democratic systems, there is less local input to objectives and policies. This can create problems if local information is required to guide a policy.

Democracies usually give more voice to localities. But even in democracies, some local governments perform far better than others. This rich variation should give social scientists plenty to say about what works and what does not. Unfortunately, that is not the case: thus far, the variety of cases is bewildering rather than revealing.

Regional diversity has its advantages, however. If different parts of the country try different things, they can learn from each others' successes and mistakes. Demonstration effects can be a powerful stimulus for reform, as can competition between regions. For this reason, the spread of the mobile phone and the extension of information technology to large numbers of people may have an enormous influence on governance. This technology makes it easier for people to know what is happening next door, or on the other side of the country, inviting them to draw comparisons.

The Environment and Energy Use

It is only a slight exaggeration to say that most developing countries decide to grow first and worry about the environment later. This is a costly mistake. Developing economies are diversifying quickly and investing heavily. In doing so, they respond to price signals. But those prices rarely reflect environmental costs. As a consequence, their investments will be misguided. Industry will install the wrong equipment and locate in the wrong places. Buildings will be designed without due regard to the energy they consume. It is costly to reverse or ameliorate these mistakes; cheaper not to make them in the first place.

It is important to emphasize that developing countries do not have to adopt the most advanced environmental standards immediately. These standards may be unaffordable. But they should plan the evolution of the economy with the environmental costs in mind.

In many parts of the developing world, energy is subsidized. This is also a mistake. According to research by IMF economists, Indonesia and Yemen spent more on fuel subsidies in 2005 than on health and education combined.[29] Although removing the subsidies is politically difficult, the costs of not doing so are high—and rising as the price of energy climbs. The cost is not only fiscal. These subsidies also distort the evolution of the economy, making energy-intensive industries artificially attractive. Moreover, as the

---

29 Coady, David, et al. 2006. "The Magnitude and Distribution of Fuel Subsidies." IMF Working Paper 06/247. International Monetary Fund, Washington, DC.

world mobilizes to combat climate change, these subsidies contribute to the problem. They may also hamper countries in their trade negotiations with the developed world, where some people now argue for higher tariffs to offset these carbon subsidies.

Environmental safeguards should not be seen simply as a concession the developing world makes to the developed. The poor suffer the most from many kinds of pollution. Effluents contaminate rivers in which the poor bathe and obtain drinking water; particulates thicken the air in neighborhoods where the poor live. Early attention to environmental standards serves the interests of equity as well as growth.

Once governments have decided to tackle this problem, they face a choice of how to do it. They can impose quantitative limits on effluents, raise prices on pollution, or issue a fixed number of tradable licenses, which give their holder the right to emit a given amount of pollution, sulfur dioxide, for example. Prices or tradable permits are efficient: they encourage polluters to find the cheapest way to cut effluents. The disadvantage is that it may take several iterations before acceptable targets are hit. Direct, quantitative caps have the opposite advantages and disadvantages: they limit effluents with greater certainty, but also at a greater cost.

Effective Government

In the first part of this report we dwelled at some length on the art of policy making. But government is not only a policy maker. It is also a service provider, an investor, an arbitrator, and an employer, often a big one. And while a government's choice of policies matters a great deal, it is also important that it implement those policies well. That is the issue to which we now turn.

The effectiveness of government depends on the talent it can attract, the incentives it fosters, the vigor of its debates, and the organizational structures it imposes. Some of the fast-growing economies prided themselves on their cadres of highly trained, well-paid civil servants, often recruited by competitive selection. An elite civil service may not come cheap. But poorly motivated, ill-prepared civil servants are tremendously costly.

Recruiting the right people is a start. Those recruits must then be given the right incentives. Otherwise, their carefully selected talents will be devoted to turf wars, office politics, or self-dealing.

That last vice—corruption—must be fought vigorously and visibly. Government leaders send powerful signals about values and the limits of acceptable behavior when they decide on how to respond to cases of misbehavior. Mild responses send the clear signal that while the misbehavior is not right, it is not all that serious. In other cases, leaders go out of their way to name and shame offenders, thus sending a clear message to others.

One way to sharpen incentives for good performance is to award promotions and salary increases on merit. But how is a civil servant's merit to be judged? If too much discretion is left to his or her superiors, they will be free to dispense promotions as patronage to their favorites. This is a legitimate concern, which explains why many bureaucracies spurn meritocracy in favor of rigid seniority systems that hand out promotions based on years of service. Such a system leaves no room for favoritism, at the cost of leaving little room for initiative either.

A better solution is to develop more objective measures of a civil servant's performance, which can be used to confirm or question a superior's judgment. Such metrics are being devised. India, for example, has invented a quality standard for bureaucracies similar to the business quality standards formulated by the International Organization for Standardization. This is one of several areas in which civil services around the world could probably learn from experiments in other countries. Although they may be reluctant to believe it, taxpayers might benefit from allowing their public servants the occasional trip abroad to exchange ideas at international training institutes and the like.

The civil service as a whole should also be held to regular account. Unlike other professions, the bureaucracy does not face a competitive test in the marketplace each day. As a result, none of its functions or lines of activity are weeded out by competitive failure. They can instead survive long into obsolescence.

Where the government provides a service, it should be forced to compete with alternative providers from the private or nonprofit sectors. In addition, it should collect feedback from the citizens it serves. Where this is not possible or not sufficient, bureaucracies should also be subject to periodic scrutiny by an independent evaluator.

These evaluators should aim to identify and remove some of the redundant layers that bureaucracies collect over the years.

The Quality of Debate

A country's fortunes depend on stopping bad policies as well as implementing good ones. Fallacies and follies must be identified, criticized, and rejected. Judging by the experiences of the members of the Commission and other leaders, the importance of this function should not be underestimated. Successful countries owe a lot to an environment in which all ideas, good and bad, are exposed to review and vigorous debate.

The policy-making process need not be confined to government circles. In many countries, the cast of actors is much larger, encompassing think tanks, the academy, the press, and independent review commissions. More autocratic countries may lack some of these elements, such as a fiercely independent press. This can leave such regimes vulnerable to policy mistakes that a freer debate might have uncovered and resisted.

However, there are many examples of highly successful autocracies that nonetheless encouraged vigorous debate. The high-growth cases include a number of countries that were dominated by a single party for at least part of their growth process. In all of these countries, the quality of the debate was high, although it was sometimes hidden from the public and outside world. It seems fair to conclude that successful countries differ more in the visibility of their policy debates than in their vigor.

Bad Ideas

Debates help clarify good ideas, subjecting them to scrutiny and constructive criticism. But debates can also be infected by bad ideas. This poses two difficulties for policy makers. First they must identify bad ideas, because specious proposals can often sound promising. Then, they must prevent them from being implemented. An illustrative list of "bad ideas", which are nonetheless often brought into the debate and should be resisted, is offered below. We hasten to add that just as our recommendations for good policies are qualified by the need to avoid one-size-fits-all approaches and to tailor the policies to country-specific circumstances, our list of bad policies must also similarly be qualified. There are situations and circumstances that may justify limited or temporary resort to some of the policies listed below, but the overwhelming weight of evidence suggests that such policies involve large costs and their stated objectives—which are often admirable—are usually much better served through other means.

- Subsidizing energy except for very limited subsidies targeted at highly vulnerable sections of the population.
- Dealing with joblessness by relying on the civil service as an "employer of last resort." This is distinct from public-works programs, such as rural employment schemes, which can provide a valuable social safety net.
- Reducing fiscal deficits, because of short term macroeconomic compulsions, by cutting expenditure on infrastructure investment (or other public spending that yields large social returns in the long run).
- Providing open-ended protection of specific sectors, industries, firms, and jobs from competition. Where support is necessary, it should be for a limited period, with a clear strategy for moving to a self-supporting structure.
- Imposing price controls to stem inflation, which is much better handled through other macroeconomic policies.
- Banning exports for long periods of time to keep domestic prices low for consumers at the expense of producers.

- Resisting urbanization and as a consequence underinvesting in urban infrastructure.
- Ignoring environmental issues in the early stages of growth on the grounds that they are an "unaffordable luxury."
- Measuring educational progress solely by the construction of school infrastructure or even by higher enrollments, instead of focusing on the extent of learning and quality of education.
- Underpaying civil servants (including teachers) relative to what the market would provide for comparable skills and combining this with promotion by seniority instead of evolving credible methods of measuring performance of civil servants and rewarding it.
- Poor regulation of the banking system combined with excessive direct control and interference. In general, this prevents the development of an efficient system of financial intermediation that has higher costs in terms of productivity.
- Allowing the exchange rate to appreciate excessively before the economy is ready for the transition towards higher-productivity industry.

The list above is illustrative and not exhaustive. Individual countries will have their own list of practices that appear to be desirable but are ineffective. Relentless scrutiny of policies should be an essential element in rational policy making. This due diligence needs to be doubled for policies of the type listed above.

PART 3

Growth Challenges in Specific Country Contexts

Sub-Saharan Africa[30]

Sub-Saharan Africa is enjoying its fastest growth in decades. The pace of the region's economies picked up in the mid-1990s and has grown by 6 percent a year in the past few years (see figure 8). African countries owe this growth to better microeconomic policies, more prudent macroeconomic management, a more generous volume of aid—and higher prices for their exports. In many countries, if not most, a new generation of leaders is in power, committed to growth and to more open and accountable government. Institutions have also improved in a number of cases. Botswana has a tradition of long-term planning guided by a vision for the future direction

---

30 Commission for Africa, 2005. *"Our Common Interest."* Report of the Commission for Africa. London. http://www.commissionforafrica.org; Collier, P. 2007. "The Bottom Billion: Why the Poorest Countries Are Failing, and What Can Be Done About It?" New York: Oxford University Press; and proceedings of the Commission on Growth Workshop on country case studies, which included Collier, P. 2008. "Growth Strategies for Africa." Working Paper No. 9. Commission on Growth and Development, Washington, DC; Maipose, G. 2008. "Policy and Institutional Dynamics of Sustained Development in Botswana." Working Paper No. 35. Commission on Growth and Development, Washington, DC; Kigabo, T. R. 2008. Leadership, Policy Making, Quality of Economic Policies and Their Inclusiveness: The Case of Rwanda." Working Paper No. 20. Commission on Growth and Development, Washington, DC; Iyoha, M. 2008. Leadership, Policy-Making and Economic Growth in African Countries: The Case of Nigeria." Working Paper No. 17. Commission on Growth and Development, Washington, DC; Ndiaye, M. 2008. "Growth in Senegal: The 1995–2005 Experience." Working Paper No. 23. Commission on Growth and Development, Washington, DC.

Figure 8 Real GDP Growth in Sub-Saharan Africa

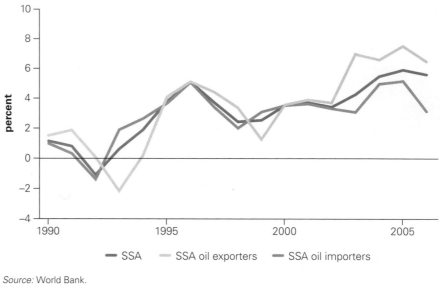

Source: World Bank.

of the economy. More recently, Rwanda has shown similar farsightedness. Nigeria, Tanzania, and Botswana have strengthened checks and balances, and have taken major initiatives toward reducing corruption. Botswana has long had a strong focus on monitoring and evaluation, and so now does Rwanda.

The challenge is to convert these favorable circumstances into lasting progress, based on rapid job growth and a more diverse economy. The task is to use the fruits of the commodities boom to reduce the region's dependency on those commodities.

Investment rates in countries such as Uganda, Tanzania, Mozambique, and Ghana are close to 20 percent of GDP or more. Over the last 10 years, these countries have lifted their saving rate and diversified their exports. But elsewhere, like many other developing countries, African economies still save and invest too small a share of their GDP. And in some cases, incentives for diversification have lessened as high commodity prices, more aid, and stronger capital inflows have strengthened their exchange rates.

Moving forward, the leadership in African countries is focused on taking advantage of the opportunity created by the commodity price increases to enter paths of higher sustainable growth. As the earlier part of this report discussed, this requires strategies facilitating integration with the global economy; densification, of people and activities; and policies that encourage self-discovery of the products in which Africa can create comparative advantage, including labor-intensive and diversified exports. This implies in turn stepped-up state involvement in infrastructure, activist and sensible industrial policies, and macroeconomic policies consistent with the need to maintain competitive exchange rates. With a view toward long-run objectives, it would also be important to formulate growth-oriented strategies with time horizons of 10 years or more.

There are several components to this effort that merit attention.

- With the help of external resources and technology, increase the productivity and output of agriculture.

- Invest in infrastructure to support agricultural productivity growth and potential export diversification as described earlier in the report. This will also help create a larger, more connected continental market.

- With the help of international development agencies, increase the productivity of private sector firms. Reduce the cost of doing business through improvements in government administration and by streamlining and simplifying administrative procedures.

- Continue the significant progress in elementary school enrollments, improve quality and the output of skills, and commit more resources to secondary and tertiary education.

- Encourage regional cooperation to build infrastructure that serves the needs of all the countries, particularly the landlocked ones.

- As many countries have low populations, they face the problems common to small states described later in this report. Regional integration to share key government services and selected outsourcing can help reduce the high per capita costs of effective government for the smaller countries.

- Promote selected financial sector development so that all citizens and sectors have access to secure channels for saving and access to credit. As in other parts of the world, progress formalizing property rights with supporting legal institutions will facilitate local investment and entrepreneurial activity, including especially the scaling-up of successful businesses.

- Adoption of best practices in the exploitation of natural resource wealth is essential in capturing and channeling natural resource rents into growth-promoting investments in education, technology, and infrastructure. The recently announced EITI++ program of the World Bank, building on the existing EITI transparency framework, has the potential to help countries manage their resource wealth. (See box 6 in the section on resource-rich countries.)

- Africa's recent macroeconomic stability owes a lot to determined policy makers and institutional reforms. Many African countries now have independent central banks. But inside and outside Africa, the origin of mismanagement has often been fiscal, not monetary. An example of what can be done is Nigeria's passage in 2007 of the Fiscal Responsibility Bill, which limits what the finance minister can do during economic cycles.

- As the investment in higher education rises, there is a growing incremental opportunity for "trade" in services, domestically and regionally, and

Box 4: Sub-Saharan Africa's geography

Africa's colonial history has left it with an unusual political geography. Although the region's 48 states vary a great deal, they can be grouped into three loose categories: coastal, landlocked, and resource-rich. Countries along the coasts of Africa can ship goods directly to world markets. Landlocked countries, on the other hand, cannot integrate easily with the world economy without the help of their neighbors. Countries in the third category may or may not lie along the coasts, but the commodities they produce are valuable enough to justify the costs of transporting them across even large distances and multiple borders.

Africa's population is distributed fairly equally across these three groups: a third, a third, and a third. This is one of Africa's most distinctive features. Outside the region, 88 percent of the devel-

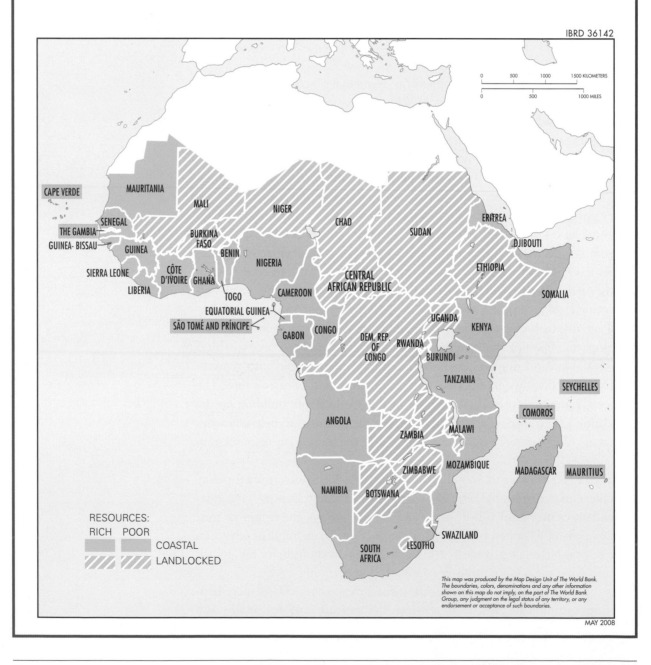

IBRD 36142

RESOURCES:
RICH POOR
      COASTAL
      LANDLOCKED

This map was produced by the Map Design Unit of The World Bank. The boundaries, colors, denominations and any other information shown on this map do not imply, on the part of The World Bank Group, any judgment on the legal status of any territory, or any endorsement or acceptance of such boundaries.

MAY 2008

oping world lives in countries with access to the coast (but no other natural resources). In Africa only a third does. Outside Africa, only 1 percent of the developing world's population lives in landlocked countries that lack natural resources. In Africa, a full third does. This configuration is the result of colonial border-making. In other parts of the world, places that are landlocked and resource-scarce did not become countries. In Africa, they did. The region cannot reverse this legacy of history. It can only try to make the best of it.

Source: Paul Collier and Stephen A. O'Connell, "Opportunities and Choices." Prepared for the synthesis volume of the African Economic Research Consortium's *Explaining African Economic Growth* project.

Note: Collier and O'Connell's paper classifies Sudan and the Democratic Republic of Congo as landlocked based on the judgment that the vast majority of the populations in these two countries have limited access to the coast.

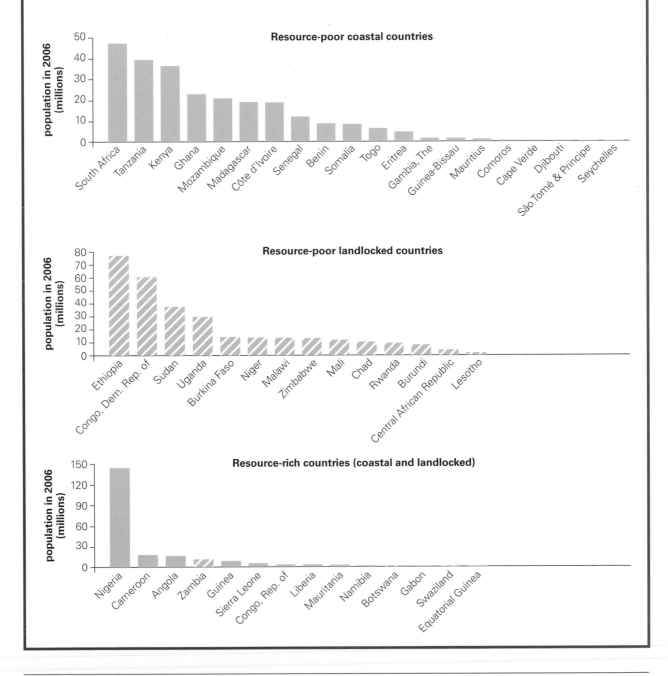

perhaps internationally. This is of particular importance to landlocked countries.[31]

- Higher education and higher-level skills training raises the brain drain issue. It is important. There is no simple response to meet this challenge. Domestic job opportunities are clearly crucial. Making public financial-support conditional on domestic employment and service is a possible approach. It has been done before. In the 1960s and 1970s in the United States, college and university loans were reduced or forgiven over time if students worked as teachers or lecturers.

It is clear that there is an expansive agenda of policy actions and investments to be undertaken, some domestically and others on a multinational basis within the continent. They will take time. Persistent, focused, and determined leadership will make the difference. It need not happen overnight. Progress on these fronts will enable a pattern of accelerated growth of an inclusive kind in the coming decades.

Africa's policy makers have spent many years preoccupied with debt, deficits, and inflation. Having won the fight for macroeconomic stability, they can now afford to think about long-term growth. Over the past two years, for example, South Africa has invited economists to visit the country and help the authorities rethink their growth strategy. Similar efforts are underway in other countries, including Rwanda, Ghana, Uganda, and Madagascar. This is important.

The foundations of sustained growth will take time to build. But the region is now blessed with a group of leaders who recognize the importance of a stable climate for private investment and clean, inclusive government. They each evince a greater sense of control over their country's destiny, and a greater sense of responsibility for it.

African countries have much to do for themselves. What can advanced countries, other developing countries, donors, and the international development institutions do by way of support?

- Grant time-bound trade preferences to manufactured exports from African countries to help them overcome the disadvantages of being late starters. If they are successful, preferences will not cost the advanced countries much and, if not successful, the costs would be minimal (see box 5).
- Provide more support to postconflict countries. Under current strategies, peacekeepers remain until elections can be held, and then leave promptly thereafter, presumably because elections legitimize the new government. In the case of the Democratic Republic of Congo, elections were held on October 29, 2006, and the withdrawal of international peacekeepers was

---

31 Bangalore, Hyderabad, and Gurgaon in India are nowhere near a coast. They depend primarily on ICT infrastructure and services, and on the normal urban services that attract a highly educated workforce.

> **Box 5: Trade preferences for Africa**
>
> Can trade preferences make a tangible difference to Africa? They already have. In October 2000, America opened its markets to 37 countries in Sub-Saharan African under the Africa Growth and Opportunity Act (AGOA). The duty-free access provided by the act has increased apparel exports to America 7- to 10-fold by some estimates. In Lesotho, for example, the garment industry accounts for almost 90 percent of the country's export earnings.
>
> The act has been less of a boon to other manufactured products, however, because they do not benefit from the same liberal rules of origin that apply to apparel. These rules determine whether a product made in one country from parts made in another, qualifies for duty-free access or not.
>
> What Africa needs is a policy giving all African countries (not only the poorest) preferential access to OECD countries, with no rules-of-origin requirements, for a period of 10 to 15 years.

scheduled for October 30. Yet the evidence suggests the risk of conflict goes up after elections, not down. Peacekeeping in fragile countries must be guided by more realistic expectations.

- Industrialized countries benefiting from Africa's brain drain need to pay for at least a part of the investments made by African governments. This could take the form of financing expansion of tertiary education.

- Rethink how aid is channeled into Africa. Over the last few decades, Africa has received a large volume of aid, in various forms. Much of this assistance has been very beneficial and has helped improve Africa's health and education status. But it does not always reflect the right priorities, or the priorities of the countries that are supposed to benefit from it. Neglected areas include infrastructure and higher education. Some also fear that large volumes of aid undermine the competitiveness of Africa's exports, either by driving up the exchange rate or bidding up local wages and prices. These fears are difficult to prove, but equally difficult to dismiss. Some argue that if aid makes the economy more productive, it will offset any harmful effects on the exchange rate. But these offsetting increases in productivity would have to be large and rapid. There is no agreement on how best to deal with this problem. But it is no excuse for donors to reduce volumes of aid. The government of a poor country may well consider the competitiveness of its export sector when choosing how much aid to accept. But that should not determine how much aid is offered.

Small States

There are over 50 small states in the world: each has a population of less than 2 million and their combined population totals less than 20 million.

Their cases are interesting in their own right. But they also help to illuminate the role of size in a growth strategy, and the potential of regional integration to make a larger economic bloc out of discrete political units.

Small states face at least three distinctive disadvantages. One is the absence of scale economies, both in the production of goods and the provision of public services. A second is risk: many small states are in regions vulnerable to hurricanes, cyclones, droughts, and volcanic eruptions. Their economies are also less diversified than those of bigger states. Some, but not all, small states are also geographically remote, a third disadvantage that makes it harder for them to integrate with the world economy.

But small states do not have lower average incomes or slower growth than other countries. Indeed, they benefit from some countervailing advantages. They are easier to monitor and comprehend, which allows policy makers to rely more on common sense and discretion. They also have little choice but to turn outward. The ratio of trade to GDP in small states is higher than for other country groups. Singapore, for example, embraced export-led growth only after the 1965 breakup of its brief union with Malaysia.

Singapore (which now has more than 2 million people) shows that smallness is not a decisive handicap in economics, especially if the country enjoys close proximity to world markets and a privileged geographical location. The expansion of world trade makes a big domestic market less vital for development. It may explain why the number of independent countries has increased rapidly in the past six decades.

In recent years, the external environment has become both more hospitable to small states and less so. A new range of services has become tradable, thanks to advances in information, communications, and technology (ICT), as the rise of outsourcing and offshoring illustrate. This creates new opportunities, which should be seized, for small countries that rely heavily on trade. On the other hand, many small states are suffering from "preference erosion." They enjoy preferential access to developed country markets, but these privileges lose their value as tariffs fall across the board. Tighter regulation of offshore financial centers has also curtailed the freedom of action of some small states.

It is noteworthy that most small states are very "young" states—over half of them were founded after 1970. Independence meant that public services, such as security, justice, and regulation of economic activity, were no longer imported from colonial powers. They instead had to be produced locally by national institutions. But the provision of such goods in small states is expensive whenever there are indivisibilities in production.

The financial system provides one example. As empires fragmented, financial transactions once contained within a single banking system had to be carried out in different currencies, under different supervisory regimes, and so on. Unfortunately, the cost of bank supervision is probably similar for a country with a population of 400,000 people as for a country with a population of 4 million. (It is certainly more than a tenth of the amount.)

In response, small states have shown great ingenuity in pooling their efforts and outsourcing public services. The Central and West Africa region, for example, relies on multicountry central banking, as does the Eastern Caribbean. The Eastern Caribbean also has a single telecommunications authority. Its Supreme Court is a particularly interesting example. It is a superior court of record with nine members. These include six independent states—namely, Antigua and Barbuda, Dominica, Grenada, St. Kitts and Nevis, St. Lucia, and St. Vincent and the Grenadines—and three British Overseas Territories: Anguilla, the British Virgin Islands, and Montserrat. As well as pooling its services, it also outsources the role of the final appellate court to the Privy Council in London.

In all of these cases, small states sacrificed some political sovereignty in exchange for better quality of service. The rules governing these arrangements were not easy to write—they had to maintain political stability and uphold high technical standards. But the consensus is that they have worked.

By contrast, Australia Aid is dealing with a dozen microstates in the Pacific, which possess many of the institutions typical of a large country: representatives in the UN, embassies abroad, central banks, and so on. In these circumstances, undiluted sovereignty is an expensive proposition. A more viable model would be a self-governing structure in association with Australia or New Zealand. One possible model is Puerto Rico, a self-governing commonwealth in association with the United States.[32]

In sum, small states should seek to pool their markets, through regional economic integration, and to spread the burden of public services, through partial political union. Good governance is an important foundation on which regional cooperation and multinational integration can build.

Dealing with risk is more difficult. In principle, it is a problem the international financial system exists to solve. A state could hold a diversified portfolio of financial assets, even if it does not have a diversified economy. But in practice, small states are more often saddled with foreign liabilities than cushioned by foreign assets. The global financial industry and the international financial institutions should be able to create instruments of interest to them. For example, Caribbean states, with the help of donors, have created an insurance fund for members struck by hurricanes or earthquakes. Their reserve pool is reinsured in the international financial markets.

Finally, small size translates into a relatively weak voice in international trade negotiations. The WTO, other international organizations, and the advanced countries need to make a special effort to take into account the

"The country I'm from, St. Lucia, has 160,000 people. The cost of government per capita is very high; the markets are very small; and the cost of production is very high. Also, every year we have a hurricane season, which can destroy the country's GDP. In some countries, it can also lead to high debt levels. Their infrastructure is destroyed, before they have paid for it, so they borrow again. Then it is destroyed a second, and sometimes even a third time."

—Sir K. Dwight Venner

---

32 For a description of the division of functions, see http://welcome.topuertorico.org/government.shtml.

peculiar needs and interests of small states. Even if their economies are not overwhelmingly significant, these states are morally and often strategically important.

Resource-Rich Countries

Thanks to burgeoning global demand for commodities, from iron ore to soybeans, countries blessed with natural resources are growing quickly. But the sudden increase in commodity prices can make it harder to diversify an economy—harder to create room for export industries that do not rely on nature's patrimony.

The foreign exchange such exporters earn counts for less in an economy flush with petrodollars or mineral revenues. And as the proceeds of commodity sales percolate through the domestic economy, wages and rents will rise, making it harder for the country's other export industries to compete abroad.

This problem of "Dutch disease," as economists call it, is not insurmountable. An endowment of natural resources did not stop several countries—Botswana, Brazil, Oman, Indonesia, Malaysia, and Thailand—from making our list of 13 success stories. Botswana's growth began before the discovery of diamonds and continued after it. Many middle-income and advanced economies have also taken resource booms in their stride. The problem is not the resources themselves, but how the proceeds (or "rents") are handled.

Governments, especially in poorer countries, do not always handle them well. In the first place, they sometimes fail to claim their rightful share of them, by selling extraction rights too cheaply and taxing the revenues too lightly. As Paul Collier of Oxford University has pointed out, the Democratic Republic of Congo received only $86,000 in mineral royalties in 2006. It is such instances that the EITI initiative (see box 6) seeks to combat.

Second, the money that does materialize is sometimes stolen or wasted. Often, it is collected and spent in secret, making it difficult to know how it is used. Resource rents have the potential to relax constraints on growth and development, providing a ready source of foreign exchange a country might otherwise lack. But they can also distort a country's politics. Political leaders may fight for power not to serve the country, but to get their hands on the resource revenues, which they can then use to buy votes and stay in power. In extreme cases, the availability of rents can lead to violent conflict over how they are spent.

Even if a government does have the right intentions, it is not easy to know how to use the money to lift growth. For example, there is no straightforward way to decide how the proceeds should be distributed over time, how much should be consumed and how much invested for the future. If governments spend the money on public investment, they need to pick the right

Box 6: The Extractive Industries Transparency Initiative

It takes the most sophisticated prospecting technologies to discover fresh oil deposits hidden beneath the earth's surface. Too often, tracking oil revenues is equally difficult. The Extractive Industries Transparency Initiative (EITI), launched in 2002, aims to bring the money that governments earn from oil, gas, and mining to the surface (www.eitransparency.org).

To meet the initiative's standards, companies must declare how much they pay to governments in royalties and for oil, gas, and mining rights. By the same token, member governments must disclose the revenues they receive from their natural resources. A big gap between those two figures would be one sign of malfeasance. Moreover, by bringing the money to light, the initiative makes it easier for outside observers to monitor its subsequent use.

The initiative is unusual in that it is managed by a broad coalition of governments, companies, industry associations, investors, the World Bank, and nongovernmental organizations like Transparency International and Global Witness. The initiative is voluntary, but it is nonetheless hard to ignore. Its reporting template provides a useful benchmark and rallying point for public campaigns and international pressure. Companies and governments that comply with its standards win public approval; those that refuse risk opprobrium. As a result, 22 countries are now implementing the initiative.

The World Bank recently announced an extension of the framework called EITI++. It aims to promote similar standards of transparency up and down the full supply chain, from the initial allocation of extraction rights to the final expenditure of the proceeds. It could, for example, help governments design auctions, monitor royalty collections, and hedge against price volatility. It could also give countries broad guidelines about how much of their revenues to spend and how much to save.

The initiative is far more ambitious than the original EITI and its success will also depend on building a broad coalition of partners and supporters. But given the extraordinary boom in commodity revenues, the stakes could not be higher.

---

projects generating the best social returns. They do not always have the capacity to do this, particularly in the early stages of development.

How, then, should governments proceed? Below we briefly describe the key elements of a sound strategy. All require governments and companies to remain open and transparent, disclosing the sums they pay and spend so the nation knows where its wealth is going.

First, governments must decide how to allocate the rights for exploration and development of their oil fields, mineral deposits, and so on. They must also decide how to tax the earnings the concessionaire makes. These two decisions together determine the flow of rents to the country and how those rents adjust to changing global prices. There is a growing body of expertise on both the design of auctions and approaches to taxation that can be tapped. That expertise should help governments strike better deals in the future. But what about the past? In cases where the allocation of exploitation rights was flawed, governments should renegotiate the concession to restore a proper balance between private return and public revenue.

The next issue is where should the rents flow? There is a plethora of options. The money can be consumed at home, or invested at home, either by the private sector or the public sector. Alternatively, it can be invested in overseas deposits, bonds, or other financial instruments. These choices will determine how the rents are distributed across generations. The calculations can become quite complicated and there is a need for a simplified framework to guide sensible choices. Because public investment matters so much to growth, and because it is often squeezed by other fiscal pressures, we would propose that it enjoy a first claim on resources. Although countries will differ in their circumstances and in the investments they choose, they should aim to invest in the range of 5–7 percent of GDP—or more if they have great needs in education or infrastructure.

Those are big sums. To get the most out of the money, governments must pick the right investment projects for the right reasons. They may need international assistance, especially with the procurement process, which is often a source of waste and corruption. Some also argue that projects should be planned, implemented, and monitored by separate parts of the government. When these functions are all combined in the same ministry, its pet projects are not questioned and mistakes are glossed over.

If these public investments do not exhaust the resource rents, the remainder should flow into a savings fund. The fund should be managed by experienced investment professionals operating within well-defined parameters of risk, return, and diversification. They should divide the money between domestic and foreign assets as best serves their investment goals. However, the capacity of the domestic economy to absorb this investment will be limited. In such cases, a nontrivial fraction of the incremental rents should be invested outside the country.

The fund must be insulated from political forces. There are two reasons for this. First, this is the only way to ensure decisions are made in pursuit of risk-adjusted returns. Otherwise, powerful interest groups will divert the investment for their own purposes. Second, there is a growing unease about the financial power of sovereign wealth funds. If a fund has political objectives that trump its commercial aims, its access to the global capital markets may in future be curtailed.

The fund should not hoard its wealth entirely. It should pay out a percentage of the total each year for the benefit of the citizens, much as nonprofit endowments do. It can pass this money to citizens directly, or do it indirectly through tax cuts. The distribution of these payouts will vary from one country to the next, but in all countries they can further the goals of equity and inclusion.

Middle-Income Countries

Of the 13 high-growth cases, six eventually reached income levels associated with the advanced countries. But this is uncommon. In a large group of

> *"Institutions—that is, organizations, norms and rules—provide sustainability and longevity to policies. Let's say you have a windfall, and there are no institutions. People tend to take the windfall as normal, and then when the windfall disappears, they have difficulty adapting. If you have institutional arrangements, I think those problems could be mitigated. They won't go away, but you won't have large swings."*
>
> *—Sir K. Dwight Venner*

countries, including many in Latin America, growth has slowed markedly at the middle-income level. The reasons are complex. If anything, this second stage of growth, from middle to high income, is less understood, and certainly less studied, than the first stage.

The focus on poorer countries is entirely understandable. But middle-income transitions deserve more attention than they have received. Many people live in such countries, including many who are poor. In a number of them, inequality remains high. The politics of a country that has lost its growth momentum are fraught. Without growth, unequal societies become trapped in zero-sum games.

No one can identify all the reasons why some economies lose momentum, and others don't. But there are common patterns across countries that are suggestive. As the economy evolves from middle to high income, it branches out into more capital-intensive and skill-intensive industries. The service sector grows. The domestic economy with its increased size and wealth becomes a more important engine of growth.

The supply of labor in middle-income countries, which once seemed infinitely elastic, ceases to be so. As surplus labor disappears, the opportunity cost of employing a worker in one sector rather than another, rises. Firms compete for workers and wages increase. These higher wages slow the growth of the labor-intensive sectors. Indeed, these export industries, which once drove growth, decline and eventually disappear.

Shortages of high-skilled labor emerge. As a result, policies shift toward promoting human capital and technology. The policy maker's role must also change. When a country is far behind the leading economies, says Philippe Aghion, a leading growth theorist at Harvard University, "it is very clear what you have to do, so you can run things like an army." But as an economy catches up with the leaders, it becomes less obvious what it should make and where its prosperity lies. More must be left to the bets of private investors and the collective judgment of the market.

The different stages are not cleanly delineated in time. In a country like China, the skill-intensive sectors, which are emerging strongly, live side by side, in a sense, with the labor-intensive industries that are still busily absorbing China's rural millions. China's policy makers show an intense determination to expand higher education and research, in response to the growing demand for human capital.

The first priority for policy makers is to anticipate this transition and the new demands it will make of them. Many governments have a planning unit, which focuses attention on the future evolution of the economy and anticipates the public policies and outlays needed to support it. Korea, for example, changed its policies and public investments in the 1980s and 1990s to help the economy's evolution from labor-intensive manufacturing to a more knowledge- and capital-intensive economy. It opened the door to foreign direct investment, privatized the national steel company, joined the OECD, and watched labor-intensive manufacturing move to new destinations.[33]

The second—not easy—is to let go of some of their earlier policies, even the successful ones. To be specific, special export zones, heavily managed exchange rates, and other forms of industrial policy can be pursued for too long. The problems these policies address decline over time, so they are not needed forever. Resisting such forces will delay the structural change of the economy. It will divert investment away from new export industries and from industries that serve the domestic market.

Singapore, for example, responded to evolving economic conditions at home and abroad by allowing labor-intensive manufacturing to migrate elsewhere in the region, where labor was cheaper. It even ran special economic zones in China and India, which hosted some of the departing industries. This allowed Singapore to concentrate its resources on industries befitting a labor-scarce economy.[34]

Just as it is possible to hold on to a labor-intensive strategy for too long, it is possible to abandon it as a growth engine too quickly. Countries should wait until surplus labor is absorbed and the human capital stock has risen to a level that supports the transition to higher value-added sectors. The effect of a premature shift can be to strand unskilled labor in traditional or informal sectors.

---

33 Nike plants for example, departed for cheaper locations elsewhere, where they were still often run by the original Korean owners and managers.

34 For an instructive discussion of the transition, see Ying, Tan Yin et al. 2007. "Perspectives on Growth: A Political Economy Framework (The Case of Singapore)." Case Study, Commission on Growth and Development.

PART 4

New Global Trends

This fourth and final part of the report turns to new global trends—features of the landscape that a developing-country policy maker cannot hope to control alone, because they are the aggregate result of many countries' behavior. These trends are also relatively new developments, which the 13 success stories did not themselves have to face. The first is the threat economic growth poses to the world's climate—and the threat the climate poses to growth.

Global Warming

Suppose the developing world does emulate the growth of China, Indonesia, and the rest of our 13 successes, industrializing briskly for the next 20 years at a growth rate of about 7 percent annually. This would be a triumph, but a qualified one. It would carry one unsettling implication: such rapid industrial expansion would add dangerous amounts of carbon dioxide to an atmosphere already polluted by unsafe concentrations of greenhouse gases (GHGs).

The Quantitative Challenge

The Inter-governmental Panel on Climate Change (IPCC) has calculated that a relatively safe level of CO_2 emissions globally is 14.5 gigatons per

Table 2 Global carbon footprints at OECD levels would require more than one planet[a]

	CO$_2$ emissions per capita (t CO$_2$) 2004	Equivalent global CO$_2$ emissions (Gt CO$_2$) 2004[b]	Equivalent number of sustainable carbon budgets[c]
World[d]	4.5	29	2
Australia	16.2	104	7
Canada	20.0	129	9
France	6.0	39	3
Germany	9.8	63	4
Italy	7.8	50	3
Japan	9.9	63	4
Netherlands	8.7	56	4
United Kingdom	9.8	63	4
United States	20.6	132	9

Source: UNDP, Human Development Report 2007, calculations based on Indicator Table 24.

a. As measured in sustainable carbon budgets.
b. Refers to global emissions if every country in the world emitted at the same per capita level as the specified country.
c. Based on a sustainable emissions pathway of 14.5 Gt CO$_2$ per year.
d. Current global carbon footprint.

year, which comes out to 2.25 tons per person per year globally. Table 2 from the United Nations Human Development Report (2007) gives the per capita emissions for major industrial countries.

Clearly the advanced countries are at per capita output levels that, if replicated by the developing world, would be dramatically in excess of safe levels. World carbon emissions are now at about twice the safe level, meaning that if the current output is sustained, the CO$_2$ stock in the atmosphere will rise above safe levels in the next 40 years. The figures for a range of countries, including developing countries, are shown in Figure 9.

If the developing countries did not grow, then safe levels of emissions would be achieved by reducing advanced country emissions by a factor of two or a little more. But with the growth of the developing countries, the incremental emissions are very large because of the size of the populations. To take the extreme case, if the whole world grew to advanced country incomes and converged on the German levels of emissions per capita, then to be safe from a warming standpoint, emissions per capita would need to decline by a factor of four. Reductions of this magnitude with existing technology are either not possible, or so costly as to be certain of slowing global and developing country growth.

What these calculations make clear is that technology is the key to accommodating developing country and global growth. We need to lower the costs of mitigation. Put differently, we need to build more economic value on top of a limited energy base. For that we need new knowledge.

Population growth is sometimes viewed as the problem. It may be in the future, but most of the projected emissions growth is not in high-

Figure 9 Per Capita CO$_2$ Emissions

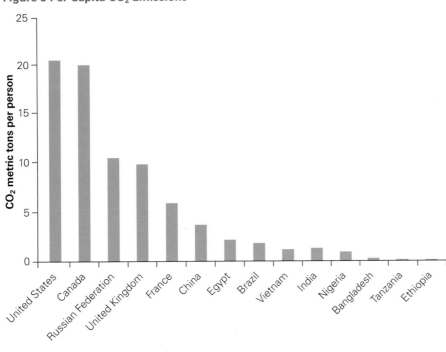

Source: UNDP, Human Development Report 2007.

population-growth countries. The real challenge is accommodating high-speed economic growth in what are currently large populations.

Carbon Intensity

The carbon intensities for the advanced countries and China and India measured as gigatons per trillion dollars of GDP are shown below. Carbon intensity is clearly much lower in advanced countries, even in the United States, which is very high in terms of energy consumption per person and per dollar of GDP (table 3).[35]

This decline of carbon intensity with per capita income is partly the result of a shift to value built on knowledge and human capital in the course of growth. It is also partly a result of the movement of energy- and carbon-intensive industries to lower-income countries. Often these industries export their products back to developed countries. To that extent, developing countries owe their carbon intensity not to their own consumption patterns, but to those of the developed countries. Declining carbon intensity will help but not solve the problem.

Table 3 Carbon Intensity (Gigatons of CO$_2$ emissions per trillion dollars of GDP)

Countries	Output
United States	0.46
European Union	0.29
Japan	0.19
China	1.67
India	1.30

Source: See appendix, p. 163.

---

35 This is a natural result of economic growth. The latter is accompanied by a structural evolution of the economy toward services, knowledge-intensive, value-added activities that are by nature less energy- and carbon-intensive.

The debate on global warming has generated its own terminology. "Mitigation" refers to efforts to reduce the greenhouse effect; "adaptation," to efforts to cope with the consequences of climate change. To put it simply, we mitigate so that we won't have to adapt, and we adapt insofar as we fail to mitigate.

Mitigation efforts include cutting carbon emissions by increasing energy efficiency. They might also include measures to remove carbon from the atmosphere by planting trees, for example. Deforestation and land use changes account of 20–30 percent of emissions growth, which could be considerably reduced by avoiding deforestation and expanding aforestation. Mitigation could also include attempts to offset greenhouse gases: if the outer atmosphere could be made more reflective, for instance, it would repel heat-generating radiation before it reaches the earth's surface and is trapped by greenhouse gases.

Adaptation includes irrigating fields deprived of rain, building levies against rising sea levels, or moving further inland. The term could also include medical responses to the diseases that might thrive in a warmer, wetter climate.

What is at stake for developing countries?

Some of the countries likely to suffer the worst, earliest damage from global warming are poor countries in the tropics. Models suggest, for example, that coastal erosion may threaten more than 1 million people by 2050 in the Nile delta in Egypt, the Mekong Delta in Vietnam, and the Ganges-Brahmaputra delta in Bangladesh.[36] Developing countries also lack the resources to adapt easily to global warming. They cannot afford, for example, to relocate large numbers of people from low-lying areas.

But developing economies are not only potential victims of climate change. Some also contribute to the problem. China, India, and other big, fast-growing economies now generate too much carbon dioxide to be ignored. China's annual emissions, for example, now approximately match those of America. The world will not succeed in its efforts to mitigate global warming if the bigger, faster-growing economies do not take part.

As a result, China, India, and their peers are under pressure to commit to cut emissions by a given percentage by 2050. They are resisting, because such commitments might threaten their growth, and also because they consider them unfair. The commitments they are being urged to make ignore the fact that their per capita emissions are much lower than those in developed economies. An equal emissions entitlement per person is, in their view, the minimum requirement for fairness.[37]

> *"Climate-change agreements need to find a way to accommodate the growth in developing countries. We don't want to say, 'I'm sorry, you arrived late. The world's changed; you don't get to grow.' It just isn't right."*
>
> —*Michael Spence*

---

36 IPCC. 2007. "Coastal Systems and Low-Lying Areas" in *Climate Change 2007: Impacts, Adaptation and Vulnerability.* Cambridge, UK: Cambridge University Press.

37 The Indian Prime Minister Dr. Manmohan Singh has stated that India would be willing to undertake to keep its per capita emissions below those of industrialized countries thus giving the latter a strong incentive to reduce their emissions as quickly as possible.

It is not wise to seek long-term commitments from developing countries to reduce emissions, nor is it likely to result in an agreement. There remains a great deal we do not know about the impact of climate change and the cost of cutting carbon. This uncertainty will be resolved over time. Therefore, the world should not lock itself into precise, quantitative commitments for the far-flung future. It should instead anticipate that information will improve—and leave some options open. Interim mitigation targets, set at periodic intervals, would allow policies to respond to new information as it arrives.

We know that the world will get warmer as a result of a given stock of GHGs. But we cannot say how much warmer with any precision. Nor do we know the costs of cutting emissions. These costs will vary by source—it may be cheaper to cut transport emissions or power station emissions—and by location—it may be costlier to cut CO_2 in Asia or in Africa. The cost of carbon cuts will also change in the future, as new clean technologies emerge.

Faced with these uncertainties, it is not wise for a country to tie its hands. But the risks for poor countries are greater. If GHGs turn out to warm the climate less than we thought, or the cost of cutting carbon turns out to be far greater than we thought, developing countries may regret any long-term promises they made.

The effort to cut carbon by a given percentage should be judged by two criteria: is it efficient? That is, are we cutting carbon as cheaply as possible? Second, is it fair? Is the mitigation effort giving room to the aspirations of developing economies to raise their living standards?

If one assumes that each country must bear the cost of its own fight against carbon, no deal will pass these two tests. An efficient agreement will be unfair, because efficiency will require carbon cuts in the developing world. A fair agreement will be inefficient, because it is relatively costly to cut carbon in the rich world. We are in a bind.

Fortunately, there is a way out of this bind: the cost of mitigation can be decoupled from the site of mitigation. Who cuts carbon is one question; who bears the cost another. In principle, high-income countries could bear the cost of cutting carbon in developing countries. The cuts can be made efficiently; the costs distributed fairly.

There are two ways to do this: a global carbon tax, or a global allocation of greenhouse gas permits, distributed fairly, which can be bought and sold. Both put a price on carbon (which creates an incentive to invent ways to economize on it). Both result in an efficient pattern of carbon cuts.

How does a cap-and-trade system divorce cost from location? Permits are given to countries, giving them the right to emit a given amount of carbon dioxide. Enough permits are awarded to poor countries to give them room to grow. But because they can sell these permits for the prevailing carbon price, they have an incentive not to use them. If economizing on carbon is cheaper than the world price of emitting carbon, they will sell the permit rather than using it.

*"Fighting climate change
will, of course, change
the pattern of growth. It
may reduce it in some
places, but expand it in
others. For example, if
we pay people to keep
forests in place, those
payments can be used for
productive purposes."*

—*Lord John Browne*

A carbon tax does not by itself separate the cost of mitigation from the location. Countries pay their own carbon taxes. Even though they also retain the revenues, these taxes may still harm the economy. Therefore a uniform, global carbon tax would have to be supplemented by a burden-sharing mechanism that pools the revenues and transfers money from rich countries to poorer ones, according to a fair principle.

The world is not as yet ready to adopt either of these solutions. Long years of design, negotiation, and implementation await. What should countries do in the meantime?

The Commission recommends the following nine steps. Taken together, they will cut emissions, thereby staving off some of the worst dangers of global warming. They will reveal more about the cost of cutting emissions, and they will encourage new technologies that reduce these costs. These steps are also fair.

1. The advanced economies should cut emissions first and they should do so aggressively. This will slow the accumulation of carbon in the atmosphere. It will also reveal a great deal about how much it truly costs to cut carbon emissions.

2. More generous subsidies should be paid to energy-efficient technologies and carbon reduction technologies, which will reduce the cost of mitigation.

3. Advanced economies should strive to put a price on carbon.

4. The task of monitoring emissions cuts and other mitigation measures should be assigned to an international institution, which should begin work as soon as possible.

5. Developing countries, while resisting long-term target-setting, should offer to cut carbon at home if other countries are willing to pay for it. Such collaborations take place through the Clean Development Mechanism provisions in the Kyoto protocol. Rich countries can meet their Kyoto commitments by paying for carbon cuts in poorer countries.

6. Developing countries should promise to remove fuel subsidies, over a decent interval. These subsidies encourage pollution and weigh heavily on government budgets.

7. All countries should accept the dual criteria of efficiency and fairness in carbon mitigation. In particular, richer countries, at or near high-income levels, should accept that they will each have the same emissions entitlements per head as other countries.

8. Developing countries should educate their citizens about global warming. Awareness is already growing, bringing about changes in values and behavior.

9. International negotiations should concentrate on agreeing to carbon cuts for more advanced economies, to be achieved 10 or 15 years hence. These mitigation efforts should be designed so as to reveal the true costs of mitigation.

We do not know how much growth countries will have to sacrifice to cut carbon 25 years from now. If those costs are high, there will be very difficult choices to make. In the meantime, we should try to cut those costs, distribute the cuts efficiently, and spread the costs fairly.

Rising Income Inequality and Protectionism

Income inequality is rising in a surprising number of countries across the globe (see figure 10). This trend is a complex phenomenon with multiple causes: technological change, shifting relative prices, and globalization. Much of it, however, is attributed to globalization.

The result is a growing skepticism about the benefits of globalization, in developing and developed countries alike. The October 2007 Pew Survey of Global Attitudes is both telling and worrying. It clearly indicates that enthusiasm for further opening of the global economy is flagging in many advanced economies, and some developing countries as well. Only countries in East Asia buck this trend.

In political terms, these attitudes can translate easily into protectionist sentiment. For example, America's administration is finding it difficult to persuade Congress to pass bilateral trade agreements with allies like Colombia and Korea. The World Trade Organization, described as the

Figure 10 Gini Annual Change

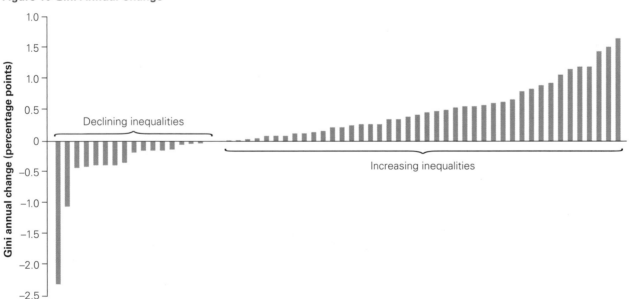

Source: World Bank, Global Monitoring Report 2008.

Note: The time period varies depending on the availability of data. Typically it is from late 1980s and early 1990s to later 1990s and early 2000s.

"The leadership of the global economy is cause for concern. A system unable to generate consensus on the Doha trade round will likely fail to reach consensus on other critical global issues such as global warming, or the rise of protectionist forces in industrialized countries."

—Montek Singh Ahluwalia

world's "insurance policy against protectionism" by its Director-General, Pascal Lamy, is likewise struggling to make progress with the Doha round of global trade talks, which were launched in Qatar in 2001 and were originally scheduled for completion by the end of 2004. Economists may disagree on the economic significance of the global deal under negotiation. But progress in the Doha round has assumed great symbolic importance as a test of the world's commitment to a flexible multilateral trading system in the face of a potential protectionist backlash.

This worrying turn in sentiment, it seems to us, is largely the result of two trends, trends that policy makers in most countries have done too little to ameliorate. One is the rapid movement of economic activity from one location to another. A second is the impact of labor-saving technologies, particularly in the sphere of information processing. Both trends add to economic growth. But both also pose a potential threat to some people's jobs and job security.

In an important sense the global economy is a public good, provision of which requires coordinated action from all countries. With enough effort from governments and international organizations, the benefits of the global economy could be distributed widely across nations and within them. The net welfare gains from openness provide ample resources to compensate globalization's casualties and discontents, if governments had the political will to manage the problem. At the moment the rhetoric is consistent with this priority, but the actions are not.

In developing countries, as noted earlier, policies designed to impede entry and exit are quite likely to succeed in slowing productivity and growth. Much the same is true in the global economy. Protecting companies and jobs from competition will slow economic progress. A better approach is to protect people and incomes, providing support to workers between jobs and preserving their access to essential services during these transitions.

To shore up support for an open global economy, governments may have to change their domestic policies. The U.S. economy, for example, offers relatively low levels of social insurance by European standards. The tax system has become less progressive over time. Certain social functions have devolved to local government and to nonprofit organizations. Some argue this provides a better balance between social insurance and protection on the one hand, and flexibility and efficiency on the other.

Other people, as one would expect, take the opposite view. We only want to make the point that the balance a country strikes between flexibility and security, efficiency and welfare, is not timeless or independent of circumstances. If economic shocks become more frequent or severe, a new dispensation might be required. It would seem quite natural to think that a country's safety nets and social insurance systems need to adapt, and probably also the tax system. The alternative approach is distinctly worse.

It is to preserve domestic systems in aspic and to shy away from the global economy instead.

Such defensiveness is damaging and counterproductive. It hurts a country's trading partners in the short run, and damages the country itself in the long run. But the task of defending an open, global economy would be easier if we stopped talking about it as an obvious choice and started to admit that it is hard and challenging work. It is not easy to adapt domestic policies and coordinate international responses to a constantly shifting global terrain. It would also serve the cause if it is acknowledged at the outset that the benefits and costs fall asymmetrically across countries, and across groups of people within countries.

The Rise of China and India and the Decline of Manufacturing Prices

One does not have to spend much time listening to the concerns of poorer developing countries to discover that a major worry is how to find room in the global economy beside the giants of China and India. Developing countries (without resource wealth) typically prise their way into world markets by trading on their relative abundance of labor. But of what value is abundant labor in a world where China, and prospectively India, have an apparently overwhelming advantage in labor-intensive manufacturing?

Will the growth strategy that worked well in the past 50 years continue to be an attractive option in the future? There is evidence of a potential problem. When the Multifiber Agreement lapsed at the end of 2005, the textile industry, freed from national quotas, expanded in some countries and shrank in others. This had damaging short-run consequences in Africa and parts of Latin America, while Bangladesh, Cambodia, India, Vietnam, and of course China, did well.

No country will remain hypercompetitive in labor-intensive industries indefinitely. At some point, the country's surplus labor will be absorbed and wages will rise. But with 55 percent of China's population still living in rural areas, and 72 percent of India's, the wait could be quite long.

The efficiency and scale of Chinese manufacturing has pushed down the price of many manufactured products, relative to many other goods and services in the global economy (see figure 11). (There are exceptions. The relative price of information-technology services has probably fallen even faster.)

This decline in manufacturing prices does not mean that labor-intensive growth strategies are impossible. It does, however, imply that they are more difficult to start and less effective in elevating incomes than they were in the past. This is discouraging news for countries, many of them in Sub-Saharan Africa, hoping to follow in the footsteps of the Asian tigers and others.

Figure 11 Chinese-Led Decline in Manufacturing Prices

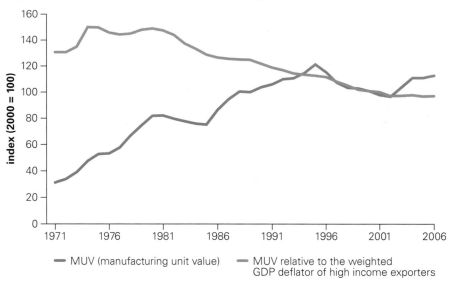

Source: Development Economics Prospects Group, World Bank.

Paul Collier of Oxford University has argued that Europe should grant African countries trade preferences, which would help them compete despite low world prices. Steps have already been taken to implement this recommendation. The advantage of this approach is that it is temporary and timely. If successful, it is not very costly to the countries granting the preferences. If it is not successful, the costs are essentially zero. These privileges, if they work, can then be extended to a wider range of poorer countries at the early stages of export diversification and growth.

Implementing trade preferences will require more flexible "rules of origin," the rules that determine such niceties as whether an African shirt made from Chinese yarn counts as African or Chinese. These rules often put such unrealistic demands on developing countries that they cannot avail themselves of the preferences they are given.

It should also be said that the global supply chains that run through countries like China and India represent a significant opportunity and not just a threat. China imports growing volumes of goods from elsewhere in Asia. These goods either serve its growing domestic market or feed the supply chains of which it is part. There is growing evidence that this new and growing demand can and will extend to other parts of the world.

The "Adding-Up" Problem

The rise of China and India has revived an old concern about export-led growth: the strategy may work for one country, but can it work for many?

If a number of economies all try to expand their exports of labor-intensive manufacturing, who will do the importing?

The question has arisen before, prompted by the rise of the four Asian tigers—Korea; Taiwan, China; Hong Kong, China; and Singapore—and the efforts of a wider range of countries to emulate their success. It was investigated by William Cline of the Center for Global Development in an influential series of studies in the 1980s. He has recently revisited the conclusions of his initial paper and subsequent book in the light of 25 more years of evidence.[38]

The problem is referred to as either the "adding-up" problem or the "fallacy of composition": what is true at the level of the individual country may not hold in the aggregate. Export-led growth may not add up for at least two reasons. One is that the glut of manufactured goods depresses prices, reducing the private and social returns to manufacturing investment. The second is that a flood of exports might provoke a protectionist response in the importing markets (largely the advanced economies), again reducing the returns to investment in these industries.

Since Cline's initial study, the original four tigers have largely exited the most labor-intensive industries. This was quite natural, a result of the tigers becoming richer and their workers becoming more expensive. It was an example of the structural evolution that underpins growth.

As they have exited these industries, China has entered, in force. Its size and growth does appear to have pushed down the relative price of manufactured goods. But there is also evidence that rising incomes are starting to push China's economy away from labor-intensive industries. Some of those industries are moving to other countries at earlier stages in the growth process. China has also emerged as an important market for capital goods and intermediate goods sold by the advanced economies, especially Japan, and the four tigers it displaced.

While the evolving pattern of trade is fascinatingly complex, there is little evidence that the point of entry available to the tigers and then to China has been blocked for later arrivals. The relative price of manufactured goods may have fallen, reducing the returns to investment in the sector. But in poor countries, where labor is cheap, those returns still exceed the cost of capital. So far, markets in the advanced economies have also remained open. However, as noted earlier, there are signs of mounting protectionist sentiment in a number of countries. We may not have heard the last word on this.

Just as some countries enter labor-intensive manufacturing, others graduate from it. There is no guarantee that the rate of exit will offset the rate of entry, so that the adding-up problem never bites. But this dynamic process of ascension and succession certainly helps. Cline notes that the

---

38 "Exports of Manufactures and Economic Growth: The Fallacy of Composition Revisited." Paper prepared for the World Bank. 2006.

potential new entrants waiting in the wings are not that large relative to global demand. In addition, China is evolving so rapidly that it may exit some industries sooner rather than later. These two facts combined reassure Cline that the labor-intensive route is unlikely to be cut off in the near future.

Cline is however concerned about a different issue, the problem of "global imbalances." Since the late 1990s, many rapidly growing economies have run trade surpluses. These surpluses were not huge, but there were a lot of them. Several developing economies, including China, also attracted large inflows of private capital. This combination of trade surpluses and private-capital inflows put upward pressure on the exchange rate, which in turn threatened the competitiveness of exports. To ward off this threat, central banks bought large amounts of dollars, which they added to their foreign-exchange reserves.

The net effect was a flow of capital to the United States, which financed America's trade deficit, allowing the country to live beyond its means. This American spending has kept the world economy ticking, but it is unlikely to be sustainable. Indeed, at the time of this report, some sort of rebalancing is already underway.

Economic growth requires a source of demand as well as supply. Over the past 10 years, America has provided more than its share of that demand. If that configuration is unsustainable, and it probably is, then growth may indeed slow as it unwinds. But other sources of demand may emerge to take up the slack. The challenge is to match the decline in the U.S. deficit with a reduction in excess saving in developing countries. Coordination is required so that the target is agreed and the time horizons match.

A number of countries already have the economic mass to make a notable contribution to global demand. And they will be joined by others, if more countries succeed in accelerating growth. Thus, it is quite possible that trade and capital flows will settle into a more sustainable pattern, which nonetheless maintains the growth rates experienced in the past decade.

The Rising Price of Food and Fuel

Food

Reversing decades of low prices, the last two years have seen sharp, largely unanticipated increases in the cost of food. Because poor people devote between half and three quarters of their income to feeding themselves and their families, the steep increase in the price of rice, grains, and edible oils is tantamount to a large reduction in their income. While in the long run higher food prices are an opportunity for those who live and work in rural areas, in the short run they create a crisis of serious proportions for the urban and rural poor, especially children. The World Bank estimates that some 100 million people may have been pushed into poverty because of the high prices of the past two years. Africa and other low-income countries are particularly vulnerable. But even middle-income countries are at risk if they lack well-developed social safety-nets.

What lies behind these steep price increases? There are many potential causes, the relative importance of which is not yet clear. The contributing factors include rising demand, shifting diets, droughts, possibly financial speculation, increased costs of key agricultural inputs such as fertilizers, and policies that encourage the use of agricultural land and output for bio-fuels. Although there is no consensus yet on the relative importance of these factors, many believe that policies that favor biofuels over food need to be reviewed and if necessary reversed.

Other longer-term factors may have been at play. Some have suggested that the low agricultural prices that prevailed until recently bred a false sense of security among governments, which led them to neglect investments in rural infrastructure, research and development, storage, and food security programs that were once a government priority. In parallel, agricultural policies in many countries encouraged nonfood over food commodities.

Whatever their cause, the high prices demand a response. The United Nations, the World Bank, and other multilateral agencies have mobilized efforts to deal with the immediate crisis by providing aid in the form of both money and food. The challenge is huge because the problem is a global one. It is unlike past episodes of starvation or malnutrition, which had local causes such as drought or conflict.

While this initial multilateral response is encouraging, the crisis has highlighted a worrying lack of economic coordination between countries, a theme to which a later part of this report returns. For example, many major food-producing countries have reacted to the crisis by restricting exports to help contain prices at home. While entirely understandable as an emergency measure, these steps exacerbate the supply shortage in the rest of the global economy, driving prices still higher. Global markets in food are becoming temporarily balkanized as a result. In the long run, this encourages countries to become self-sufficient in food, even if this is not their comparative advantage. As yet, there is little awareness of these long run risks, nor is there an adequate global mechanism for managing them.

High prices will also tempt governments to introduce price controls. These measures also are understandable and perhaps even justified in an emergency. But while governments will want to protect consumers, they also have to recognize that such interference in the price mechanism is counterproductive over the long run.

Higher prices are an important signal to domestic food producers, encouraging them to expand their supply. But not all farmers will be able to respond vigorously. Large numbers of small farmers lack the technology and the inputs needed to raise their productivity to its full potential. An

"There is no effective development strategy that doesn't first deal with the issue of hunger. But there is a distinction between food security and food self-sufficiency. Successful economies have striven for growth that gives the broadest segment of the population sufficient purchasing power to buy adequate nutrition. Without this, we cannot hope to see healthy mothers, effective students or productive workers."

—Danny Leipziger

effective supply response therefore requires sustained public investment in critical aspects of rural infrastructure, a stronger publicly funded research effort, and an expansion of credit to underserved farmers. A sustained effort at increasing food production must therefore play a larger part in the development strategy of most developing countries than it has done so far.

If farmers do eventually produce a much bigger crop, high food prices will subside. But to assume this is a one-time event is probably not a good idea. The global system is likely to be vulnerable to such shocks on an ongoing basis. It would therefore be wise to put better systems in place to respond to them. Countries urgently need effective social-safety nets that distribute cash to the poor or offer them employment on public-works programs. Reserves and inventories need to be accumulated to relieve temporary shortages, especially since persistent export bans cannot be ruled out. It is more efficient to build these buffer stocks on a multinational basis with suitable assurances of access and availability.

Fuel

Food staples are not the only commodities that have risen sharply in price in recent years. Crude oil prices have increased from under $25 a barrel six years ago to over $110 in May 2008. Many governments are understandably reluctant to allow these higher prices to pass directly to consumers. But unless buyers face higher prices they will have no incentive to economize on fuel or to shift to less energy-intensive production. Costly energy subsidies will only make societies more dependent on oil and leave governments with less money to help the poor.

One big question remains. Do these rising prices mark the beginning of a period in which natural resources, broadly defined, impose new limits on global growth? It is possible. Growth, both globally and in developing countries, may be somewhat slower than the pace set in the recent past. But it is not possible to know in advance how tight the new limits might be.

It is worth noting that knowledge and ingenuity, not oil or minerals, account for much of the value that has been added to the global economy in recent years, especially in the leading economies. If this pattern holds in the future, the amount of natural resources required to produce a dollar of GDP will continue to decline.

There are optimists and pessimists about this. But it is clear that our collective future will depend on our ability to create as much value as possible on the natural resource base that we have.

Demographics, Aging, and Migration

The global population is aging. That conclusion emerges clearly from the evidence and forecasts we reviewed with the help of some distinguished

"Rapid growth remains both possible and necessary for the billions of people throughout the developing world . . . if it can be made to be inclusive, and if it can adapt to new natural-resource and climate constraints that have to be taken seriously."

—Kemal Derviş

demographers. This aging has two principal causes: a fall in fertility and a large increase in longevity. Infants are entering the global population at a lower rate, and elderly people are exiting it later. There are of course countries and regions that do not reflect this pattern, especially poorer countries where fertility rates remain high and diseases like HIV/AIDS have reduced longevity substantially.

Nonetheless the overall pattern is clear. The question is whether this aging will have a major impact on global growth and related variables like saving and investment. These are complex issues and this is not the place to go into detail. We confine ourselves to the major conclusions and refer the interested reader to the more detailed studies.

Aging societies account for about 70 percent of global GDP, large enough to be significant. As their populations gray, must their economic growth slow? According to simple arithmetic, if the number of working-age adults stagnates or falls, and the number of retirees increases, this must surely squeeze income per head. There are fewer people to earn the income, but no fewer people to divide it among.

But this gloomy projection assumes that the definition of "working-age" remains the same as it does today. That is unlikely to be true. In many countries and regions (including most of Europe, North America, Japan, and China), the graying of the population threatens the solvency of the country's pension arrangements. As a result, reforms are needed to extend the working life in these countries, or to give people a different set of choices with respect to retirement, income, and consumption before and after retirement. The current fixed retirement ages cannot survive.

Thus the reforms needed to restore the fiscal viability of many national pension systems will also change the length and pattern of working lives. If these reforms are undertaken gradually, as we expect, then the research suggests there is no compelling reason to expect a major slowdown in global growth.

Several countries are moving away from a "pay-as-you-go" pension system, in which taxes are levied on today's working generation to pay for today's retirees. They are opting instead for more fully funded systems, in which today's working generation accumulates financial assets that will give it a claim on future output.

As countries shift from one system to another, their saving rate may increase temporarily, adding to the "savings glut" in the world economy. That shift away from consumption could adversely affect growth for a period of time.

Aging is mostly a problem for the richer countries but does include China. Many of the world's least developed countries have the opposite problem. Populations are young, and in countries ravaged by diseases like HIV/AIDs, the "anti-aging effect" is dramatic.

"In speaking about human progress, there is much to celebrate, but there is also much to deplore, because almost half of the world's people are still living in poverty. We have focused on economic growth because without it the polarization between the haves and the have-nots in our world would continue to widen and remain a cause of conflict and instability."

—Ernesto Zedillo

As a result, some countries have millions of young people leaving school and entering job markets that cannot absorb them. Moreover, as new entrants to the labor force, youth are often at a disadvantage to more experienced workers. The result is a worrying youth unemployment problem. It is a predicament that goes well beyond economics, posing a moral challenge and a security risk. And it is very widespread.

In some areas, even very high growth rates will not be quick enough to absorb the forecast labor supply. The numbers are striking (see figure 12). From now until 2050, the world is projected to add 3 billion people. Only 100 million will be in rich countries. One billion will be in fast-developing countries, like India and China. The remainder, which is to say two-thirds of the world's population increase, will be added in countries that do not yet have a solid track record of growth. Thus, the supply of labor is not where the jobs are being created.

This demographic problem cannot be solved by individual countries alone. The solution will have to span national boundaries. For many countries, it is clear to us, migration for purposes of work is the only potential solution. Workers will have to move from countries where labor is abundant to countries where it is scarce. Migration for work needs international supervision to prevent abuses in the treatment of mobile labor.

Cross-border migration is a double-edged sword for developing countries. For those with excess labor supplies, it is an opportunity. The money that migrants remit back to their families and homes now far exceeds all

Figure 12 Population Growth: 1960–2006 and 2030 Forecast

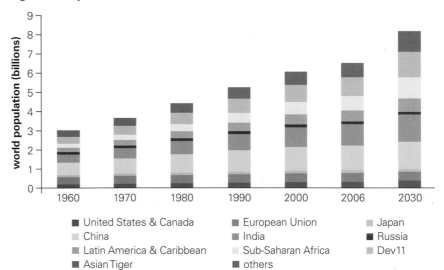

Source: World Bank, World Development Indicators 2007; Forecast for 2030 from Maddison, Angus. 2001. *The World Economy: A Millennial Perspective.* Paris: OECD.

official aid. On the other hand, many countries suffer an outmigration of highly educated people whose service in government, business, and professional sectors would benefit the home country.

The problem is compounded if the migrants were educated with public funds. The migrant enjoys the private return to this education, even as his or her home country misses out on the social returns. There are techniques for dealing with this potential divergence. One example would be to offer students loans for their education, then cut the repayment amount for every year they work in their home country.

Countries can also do a lot to win back their highly educated and experienced citizens. Fast-growing economies, where opportunities abound, can attract substantial return migration. And these skilled returnees can, in turn, make a substantial contribution to a country's growth. Homecoming and fortune-hunting can form a virtuous circle.

What about permanent migration from poor to rich countries? Large-scale migration from the developing world to the developed world would increase global incomes substantially. If the migrants were younger on average than the citizens of their host countries, it would also slow the aging of the host's population. While both statements are true, the political and social complexity associated with permanent migration on a large scale make it unlikely to occur. It should not be counted on as an important driver of inclusive growth at the global level, at least not in the near future.

Global Imbalances and Global Governance

Developing economies have become a more intrusive presence in the rich world. In the past, their economic triumphs and mishaps were noted with applause or regret. But however important developing economies were locally or regionally, they did not have large macroeconomic consequences for the world economy. It was the advanced economies that accounted for the bulk of global output, income, and assets. And insofar as the world economy was governed by anyone, it was governed by policy makers in the capitals of the rich world.

This constellation of powers is changing rapidly. The defining economic characteristic of the next few decades is likely to be the increasing size and expanding role of the developing world. China's 2007 GDP is about $3.2 trillion (at market exchange rates, with no adjustment for purchasing power parity) and growing at over 10 percent a year. It is almost 20 percent of the size of the U.S. economy, which means that 10 percent growth in China is the equivalent of 2 percent growth in the United States or Europe. India's economy is approaching $1 trillion. It is likely to follow China's path with a lag of about 12–15 years.

By mid-2007, reserves held by central banks were about $4.5 trillion. China's reserves alone are about $1.6 trillion and rising, thanks to its growing trade surplus (10–12 percent of GDP in 2007) and the heavy private capital flows it attracts (see figure 13). The holdings of sovereign wealth funds, which are on the order of $3 trillion, are also rising because of high oil prices and governments' willingness to hold a more diversified portfolio of foreign assets. Some worry that these funds, which are owned by governments, will make their investment decisions for political reasons, not just commercial ones. There is no evidence that this has yet happened on any scale. But it is in everyone's interest to make sure it does not happen, by making the right formal agreements and institutional arrangements.

Thanks to financial innovation, the stock of financial assets has grown three times faster than global GDP since 1980. But this ingenuity has also made several markets more opaque and more difficult to regulate, as the current credit crisis (2007–08) in America and Europe illustrates. These troubles have also left the financial and monetary authorities confused about their roles. The responsibilities of central banks now extend beyond inflation to credit crunches, growth slowdowns, asset bubbles, and, in some cases, exchange rates. In the face of relatively free international capital flows, it is unclear whether central banks have enough instruments to accomplish these objectives.

Since the summer of 2007, the capital markets have begun to price risky assets less generously. But the world economy is still unbalanced. United States savings rates are still low, China's reserve accumulation has not slowed, and its trade surplus, once modest, is now rising rapidly. Currencies

Figure 13 Chinese Reserves

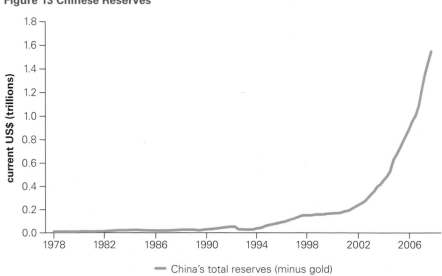

China's total reserves (minus gold)

Source: IMF, International Financial Statistics.

The Growth Report: Strategies for Sustained Growth and Inclusive Development

that track the dollar (or the yuan) have largely accompanied the American currency on its descent, in defiance of their underlying fundamentals.

It is clear to most observers that the global economy has outrun our capacity to manage it. This creates risks for developing countries in particular, because they are most vulnerable to sudden stoppages of credit, and sudden switches of international custom or supply. Wherever they are able to do so, countries are taking precautionary steps. They are amassing substantial foreign currency reserves and limiting capital flows in various categories that pose potential risks to stability, growth, and competitiveness. In the wake of America's subprime crisis, developing countries are newly skeptical of the proposition that lightly regulated capital markets work best.

Indeed, a number of developing countries have their own potential asset bubbles to worry about. The price of real estate in Mumbai, for example, is reported to be as high or higher than that of New York or London. Housing prices in many parts of the world have become detached from rents. When asset bubbles burst, they have the potential to produce rapid slowdowns in the nonfinancial economy as well.

As the number of influential countries grows, it becomes all the more important to establish a mechanism for coordinating their policies. These economies, which now include the larger developing countries, share a joint responsibility for the stability of the global financial system. But there is no international institution that allows them to discharge this responsibility properly. The G8 excludes them by design. The International Monetary Fund has tried to accommodate them, but its "quota" reforms have redistributed voting power only marginally. To many in Asia, the IMF remains a creature of a postwar age, dominated by the European and American economies, that has passed.

An international institution that gave emerging economies their due would have two tasks. First is the duty of monitoring and keeping watch, what the IMF calls "surveillance." The international system must anticipate financial strains, imbalances, and fragilities. This would allow it to act early to reduce the chances of abrupt adjustments. The second task is to muster a timely and coordinated response to those crises it failed to anticipate, such as rising food prices.

The global economy, this report has argued, made it possible for 3 billion people to enjoy the fruits of growth in the postwar period. It also provides an economic springboard for another 2 billion people to fulfill their aspirations. No doubt the global marketplace poses risks. No doubt people need to be protected from its harsher consequences and unrulier moments. But it is also true that openness itself needs protecting. An international economy in a world of nation-states has no natural guardians. That is perhaps the biggest risk of all.

Statistical Appendix
The World Economy and Developing Countries since WWII

This appendix is a graphical review of the evolution of the global economy in the postwar period and the growing role of developing countries. We present the main characteristics of developing countries' economic and social evolution, and some features of the global economic environment that influence these countries' economic prospects and challenges.

In doing this review we have been surprised by the extent to which important data on developing countries are incomplete or contradictory. On the one hand, there are basic problems such as compilation issues. For example, no single source provides time series for all countries' national accounts that are consistent with national accounts statistics: more often than not the time series are truncated. On the other hand, there are more serious problems such as lack of data. For example, data are incomplete on infrastructure and quality of education and, more generally, on the efficiency of public sector spending. It seems important that international development institutions and statistical offices invest the time and resources needed to address this problem.

The appendix consists of six parts. Part 1 reviews the evolution of GDP in industrialized and developing countries. Part 2 documents population trends, including forecasts. Part 3 deals with poverty in developing countries and some of its main characteristics. Part 4 provides some information on the evolution of socioeconomic indicators, education and health indicators in particular. Part 5 reviews selected information on infrastructure, an area where data are surprisingly incomplete. Part 6 reviews important global trends.

1. EVOLUTION OF GLOBAL GDP AND PER CAPITA GDP

1.1 Evolution of Global and Per Capita GDP in the Last 2,000 Years

A school of thought has long maintained that modern economic growth started with the "Industrial Revolution." In fact, economic growth started well before, as a result of the spread of universities in the 14th and 15th centuries, and a series of scientific and technological innovations (e.g., the printing press, progress in ship engineering, navigational instruments, and advances in meteorological and astronomical knowledge). These developments, together with the return of some peace and security in Western Europe which facilitated trade, contributed to the acceleration of economic growth before the Industrial Revolution. After several tens of thousands of years of low or negligible economic progress, growth accelerated circa 1,000 AD, accelerated again in the 19th century and, some believe, has accelerated once more in the last two decades—although it is too early to conclude on the latter. This evolution in per capita incomes is illustrated in the figure below, which shows estimates of both the world GDP and of per capita incomes in the past two thousand years.

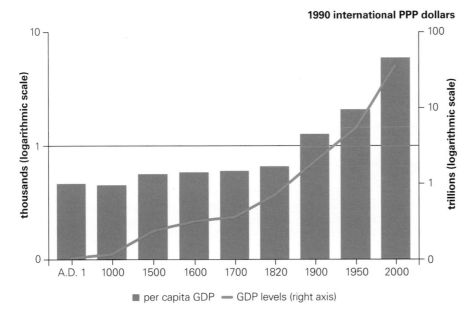

1990 international PPP dollars

Legend: ■ per capita GDP — GDP levels (right axis)

Source: Maddison, Angus. 2007. *Contours of the World Economy, 1–2030 AD.* Oxford, UK: Oxford University Press.

Note: PPP = purchasing power parity.

1.2 The Growth of the World Population and Some Major Events in the History of Technology—9,000 B.C. to Present

Growth in incomes was accompanied by unprecedented increases in population and exponential increases in the rate of scientific discoveries.

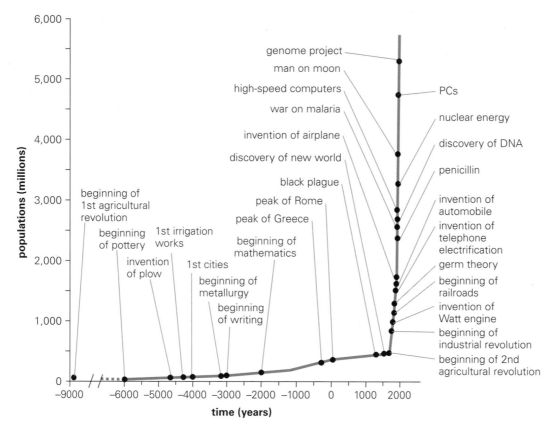

Source: Fogel, Robert. 1999. "Catching Up with the Economy." *American Economic Review* 89(1) (March): 1–21.

Note: There is usually a lag between the invention of a process or a machine and its general application to production. "Beginning" means the earliest stage of this diffusion process.

1.3 Long-Term Evolution of Per Capita GDP for Selected Developing Countries and Regions

Until WWII, economic growth was limited to Europe and North America. Per capita income stagnated elsewhere as shown in figure 1.3, where the horizontal axis measures per capita incomes for different groups of countries or regions over the past 2,000 years.

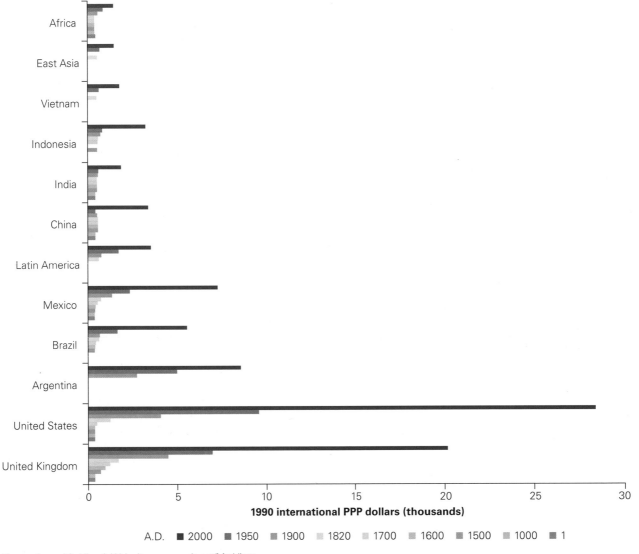

Source: Angus Maddison's Web site, www.ggdc.net/Maddison.

Note: PPP = purchasing power parity.

1.4 Global GDP since 1960

After WWII, some developing countries started to grow at high rates and to catch up with industrialized countries, thus contributing to the exponential growth of world GDP. Figure 1.4 shows how different groups of countries and regions have contributed to the world's GDP since 1960. It shows that the United States, Canada, the European Union, and Japan account for well over half the global GDP, but that this proportion has been declining as a result of China and India's growth. Since WWII Japan has experienced high growth that is a hybrid of catching up and postwar recovery. Whereas Japan was part of the developing world in the 1950s, 1960s, and part of the 1970s, it is now an industrialized economy and its GDP ranks among the world's largest.

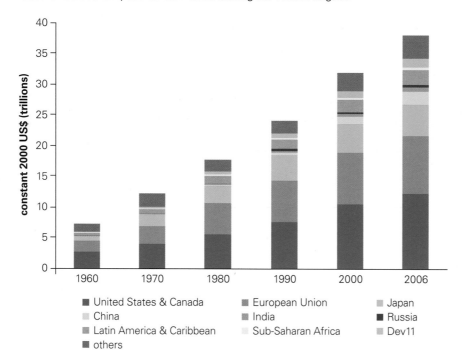

Source: World Bank, World Development Indicators 2007.

Note: As of 2006, the European Union (European Union) consisted of 25 countries. Years of data availability vary by country; for example, German GDP begins in 1971. "Dev11" refers to the 11 developing countries that are among the 25 largest developing countries featured in table 1.1 and are not captured by the categories above. Dev11 comprises Algeria, Bangladesh, the Arab Republic of Egypt, Indonesia, the Islamic Republic of Iran, Malaysia, Pakistan, the Philippines, Romania, Thailand, and Turkey. The top 10 economies in the "others" category by size are the Republic of Korea; Australia; Taiwan, China; Switzerland; Hong Kong, China; Norway; Singapore; New Zealand; Ukraine; and Vietnam.

1.5 Growth in Today's 25 Largest Developing Countries

Some of the largest developing countries have put their economies on track to catch up with industrialized countries; many others have not. There are about 150 developing countries in the world. The 10 largest account for about 70 percent of developing countries' GDP, and the 25 largest countries for about 90 percent. The growth performance of these 25 countries has been uneven. Because industrialized countries' secular growth rate is about 2 percent per capita, developing countries need to grow at much higher rates to catch up. Less than half have been able to reach this performance as indicated in the table below. Since 1960, only 6 countries have grown faster than 3 percent in per capita terms and 10 had growth rates below 2 percent, implying that they have fallen farther behind industrialized countries' incomes. Japan and the Republic of Korea are two large economies in the category of developing economies after WWII that, because of their growth performance, have reached the income levels of industrialized countries and hence are not in this table. As mentioned above, Japan's growth is a hybrid of war recovery and catching up.

	Real GDP* 2006	Share in total**	GDP growth rate***				Rank 1960	Real GDP 1960
			1980–2006		1960–2006			
			Real	Per capita	Real	Per capita		
China	2092	25.4	9.8	8.6	7.7	6.1	5	70
Brazil	765	9.3	2.2	0.5	4.4	2.3	2	105
India	703	8.5	6.0	4.1	4.9	2.8	4	77
Mexico	666	8.1	2.6	0.9	4.3	2.0	3	94
Russian Federation	373	4.5	−0.4	−0.2	–	–	–	–
Argentina	340	4.1	1.8	0.5	2.5	1.1	1	108
Turkey	261	3.2	4.4	2.5	*4.3*	*2.2*	–	–
Indonesia	219	2.7	5.2	3.6	5.5	3.6	8	18
Poland	210	2.6	*3.7*	*3.7*	–	–	–	–
South Africa	169	2.0	2.2	0.1	3.3	1.0	7	38
Thailand	165	2.0	5.9	4.5	6.6	4.5	19	9
Venezuela, R. B. de	147	1.8	2.0	−0.3	2.8	0.0	6	41
Iran, Islamic Rep. of	140	1.7	3.5	1.3	*4.4*	*1.8*	–	–
Egypt, Arab Rep. of	128	1.5	4.7	2.6	5.3	3.0	17	12
Malaysia	119	1.4	6.1	3.6	6.6	3.9	22	6
Colombia	106	1.3	3.2	1.4	4.2	1.9	11	16
Philippines	99	1.2	2.9	0.7	4.0	1.4	9	17
Pakistan	99	1.2	5.1	2.5	5.5	2.7	20	9
Chile	96	1.2	4.9	3.3	4.3	2.5	12	14
Algeria	72	0.9	2.8	0.5	3.6	1.1	13	14
Peru	71	0.9	2.3	0.4	3.2	0.9	10	16
Bangladesh	65	0.8	4.6	2.3	3.6	1.3	16	13
Nigeria	64	0.8	2.7	0.0	3.5	0.8	15	13
Hungary	62	0.7	1.7	2.0	3.4	3.4	14	13
Romania	53	0.6	1.0	1.1	–	–	–	–
Others	965	11.7	–	–	–	–	–	–

Source: World Bank, World Development Indicators 2007.

Note: The table excludes countries that were developing in 1960 and have already reached industrialized countries' income levels. Numbers in italics and red indicate different time periods due to data availability: Russia (1989–2006), Turkey (1968–2006), Poland (1990–2006), Iran (1965–2006).
*Real and per capita GDP in constant 2000 US dollars, billions.
**Shares in total developing countries' real GDP in 2006.
***Period growth rate in CAGR (compound annual growth rate).

1.6 Divergence in Economic Performance, 1960–2006

Differences in economic performance are significant. This applies particularly to Africa and Latin America, where growth has been slow or has slowed relative to the incomes of industrialized countries, implying that they have fallen behind.

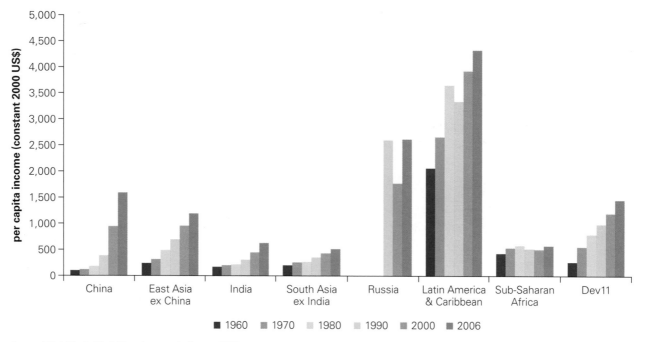

Source: World Bank, World Development Indicators 2007.

1.7 Catching Up

Another way of describing differences in developing countries' economic performance is to ask what growth rate a country would need to achieve to catch up with industrialized countries (whose per capita income is growing at the 2 percent secular rate) by a certain date. The table below shows the increase needed to catch up by 2050 and by 2100. Current trends persisting, China could reduce its per capita growth rate to 5.7 percent per year, down from its 8.3 percent average during the past 10 years. This indicates that at current rates China will catch up with industrialized countries before 2050. Brazil, on the other hand, needs to raise its per capita income growth rate by a factor of 5 compared to its 1.1 percent growth over the past 10 years to catch up with industrialized countries by 2050.

The last column in the table below shows the number of years needed for a country to catch up with OECD countries, assuming it grows in the future at the highest rate registered in the last 10 years. This rate is obviously arbitrary. Countries that experience large fluctuations, such as Venezuela, will automatically have a very high growth rate, explained by rebounds, and hence an artificially low number of years to catch up. Using the average for the last 10 years would have provided a more credible estimate. However, many countries have an average per capita growth rate for the decade well below the OECD secular per capita growth rate, implying that they would never catch up at such rates. On the other hand, the table shows that all countries grew at a rate above 2 percent in at least one year. Using this rate renders the calculation mathematically feasible, but its economic meaning needs to be interpreted carefully.

Growth has recently accelerated in countries in Africa, Latin America, and the Middle East, partly as a result of commodity price increases, and partly as a result of changes in economic policies. The issue now is whether this acceleration will persist.

	Per capita GDP* in 2006	Growth rate during past 10 yrs		Growth rate needed to catch up***		Years needed to catch up****
		maximum**	average**	in 2050	in 2100	
China	6,621	10.1	8.3	5.7	3.7	23
Brazil	7,826	4.3	1.1	5.3	3.5	119
India	3,308	7.7	4.9	7.4	4.5	50
Mexico	9,967	5.2	2.4	4.7	3.3	55
Russian Federation	10,350	10.0	5.4	4.6	3.2	17
Argentina	13,652	8.1	1.7	4.0	2.9	17
Turkey	7,842	8.3	2.7	5.3	3.5	28
Indonesia	3,570	4.3	1.3	7.2	4.4	181
Poland	13,349	7.0	4.3	4.0	3.0	22
South Africa	10,338	3.9	1.7	4.6	3.2	135
Thailand	8,065	6.2	1.8	5.2	3.5	45
Venezuela, R. B. de	6,485	16.2	1.1	5.7	3.7	13
Iran, Islamic Rep. of	7,405	5.9	3.2	5.4	3.6	54
Egypt, Arab Rep. of	4,031	4.9	2.7	6.9	4.3	118
Malaysia	10,091	6.4	2.2	4.7	3.3	35
Colombia	6,886	5.4	1.0	5.6	3.7	68
Philippines	4,731	4.3	2.2	6.5	4.1	159
Pakistan	2,206	4.8	1.8	8.3	4.9	159
Chile	10,939	5.1	2.6	4.5	3.2	54
Algeria	6,376	5.3	2.4	5.8	3.8	75
Peru	5,725	6.5	2.3	6.0	3.9	51
Bangladesh	1,916	4.8	3.5	8.7	5.1	163
Nigeria	1,008	8.0	1.8	10.3	5.8	74
Hungary	16,928	5.5	4.7	3.4	2.7	26
Romania	8,722	8.7	3.1	5.0	3.4	24

	Per capita GDP in 2006	Growth rate during past 10 yrs		Per capita GDP***		
		maximum	average	in 2050	in 2100	
OECD	30,897	3.08	2.04	75,130	206,222	–

Source: World Bank, World Development Indicators 2007.

*Per capita GDP based on purchasing power parity, in constant 2000 international dollars.
**Maximum and simple average of the annual growth rates during the past 10 years.
***Assuming growth at annual rate of 2.04%, which is the average growth rate of OECD during the past 10 years.
****Assuming both grow at the maximum growth rate achieved during the past 10 years.

1.8 Rapid Growth Is Urban Based—Decomposition of Growth Rates for the Fast-Growing Economies: Various Periods

In all cases of sustained high growth (7 percent or more sustained over 25 years or more), it is production in urban areas—that is, manufacturing and services—that led the growth.

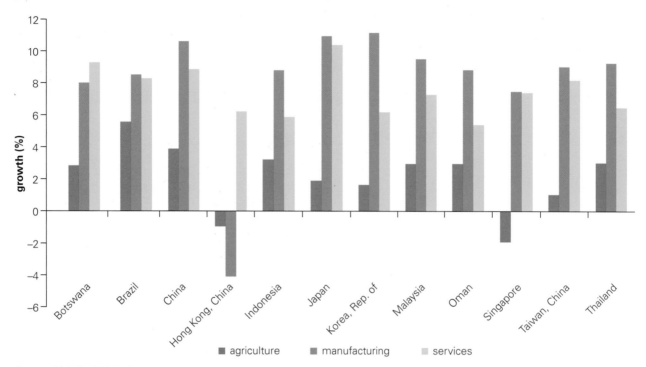

Sources: World Bank, World Development Indicators 2007; for Brazil: World Bank calculation using data from World Tables 1976, World Bank, and Institute of Applied Economic Research (IAER), Brazil (http://www.ipeadata.gov.br); for Japan: World Bank calculation using data from World Tables 1976, World Bank, and Maddison, Angus, 2001: *The World Economy: A Millennial Perspective.* Paris: OECD.

Note: The calculations apply for different periods indicated in parentheses because of different degrees of consistent data availability: Botswana (1965–2006); Brazil (1955–73); China (1965–2006); Hong Kong, China (2000–06); Indonesia (1960–2005); Japan (1955–73); Korea, Rep. of (1970–2006); Malaysia (1970–2006); Oman (1988–2004); Singapore (1975–2006); Taiwan, China (1965–2006); and Thailand (1960–2006).

1.9 Divergence in Sub-Saharan Africa and East Asia, 1960–2006

Another way of looking at divergence is to compare selected regions or economies over time. The figure below shows differences in performance of Africa overall in relation to East Asia.

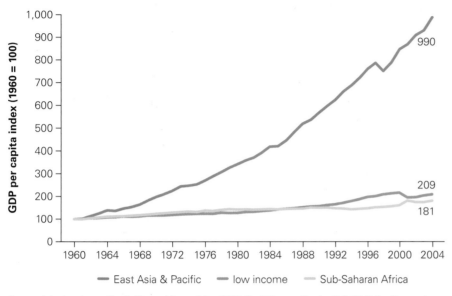

Source: Arbache, Jorge, Go, Delfin, and Page, John. 2008. "Is Africa at a Turning Point?" Policy Research Working Paper 4519, February. World Bank, Washington, DC.

1.10 Divergence within Africa, 1960–2006

Within Africa itself there has been significant divergence. For example, Mauritius and Côte d'Ivoire faced the same international market for commodities and became independent at about the same period. Mauritius pursued a growth strategy aimed at supplying the external market, integrating itself with the global economy, and diversifying its production and exports. Conversely, Côte d'Ivoire relied almost exclusively on the rents of its commodity exports. Zambia and Botswana started with about the same per capita income, and both were rich in minerals: again, different policies and institutions brought about different results.

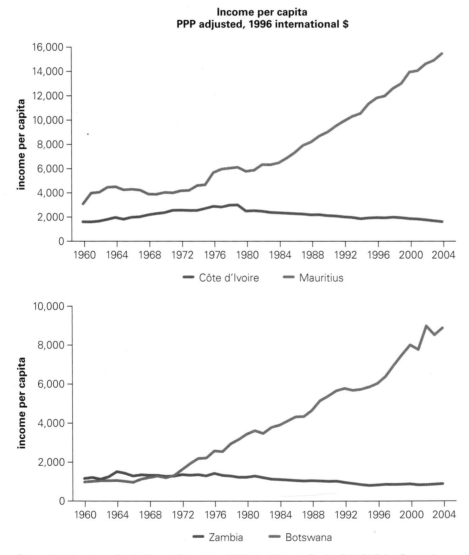

Income per capita
PPP adjusted, 1996 international $

Source: Arbache, Jorge, Go, Delfin, and Page, John. 2008. "Is Africa at a Turning Point?" Policy Research Working Paper 4519, February. World Bank, Washington, DC.

Note: PPP = purchasing power parity.

1.11 The Rise of China and India, 1960–2006

Because of the consistently improving economic performance of China and India, the share of developing countries in global GDP is increasing. The corollary is that the share of the United States, Canada, Japan, and the European Union has been declining since the 1980s—although these economic blocks together still account for 70 percent of the world's GDP.

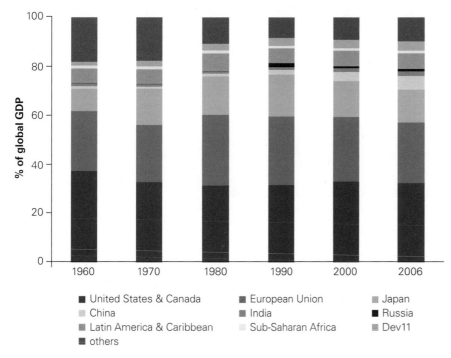

Source: World Bank, World Development Indicators 2007.

2. POPULATION: TRENDS AND FORECASTS

2.1 Population Growth, 1960–2006 and 2030 Forecast

Since WWII, most of the growth in the world's population has taken place in developing countries.

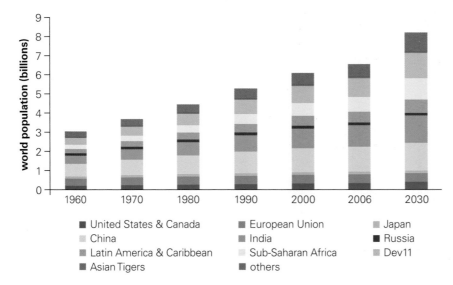

Source: World Bank, World Development Indicators 2007; forecast for 2030 from Maddison, 2001.

2.2 Global Population, 1960–2006 and 2030 Forecast, Percent Distribution

The corollary to population growth in developing countries is that industrialized countries account for a dwindling share of the world population.

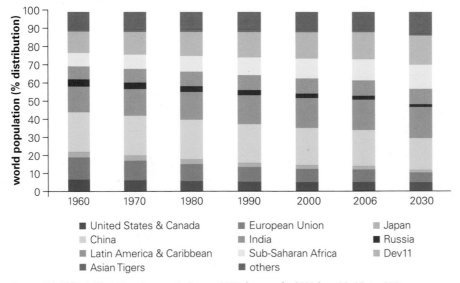

Source: World Bank, World Development Indicators 2007; forecast for 2030 from Maddison, 2001.

2.3 Demographic Change, 1950–2050, by Five-Year Age Group

The figures below illustrate for different groups of countries and regions the evolution of the age structure of the population from 1950 to present, and how it is expected to evolve from the present to 2050. The figures ignore future migration flows. Reading the age axis from left to right provides the age composition of the population at different points in time, starting in 1950, by five-year age groups. Reading the time axis from past to present, and then to the future, following the contour on the surface, shows the evolution in size of a particular age group. In the case of China, for example, as one moves right along the time axis, the figure shows first an increase in the number of children in the 0–4 year group, followed by a sharp decline, which is expected to continue throughout 2050. All the countries and regions have experienced or will experience a decline in the low age categories as a result of declining birth rates. In the case of the United States and the European Union, for example, declining birth rates explain the rise in the high age categories. One important exception is Sub-Saharan Africa, where low age groups are expected to continue to increase in number. Another exceptional feature of Sub-Saharan Africa's population trends is the expected rapid decline in population in the higher age categories.

The main conclusions of the figures below are that important demographic changes are underway that will lead to rapidly aging populations in industrialized countries.

Populations in industrialized countries will age rapidly.

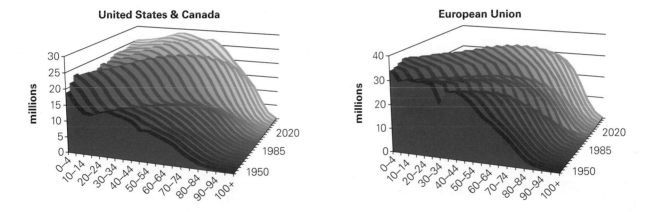

Aging will be particularly pronounced in Japan, Russia, and, to a lesser extent, China.

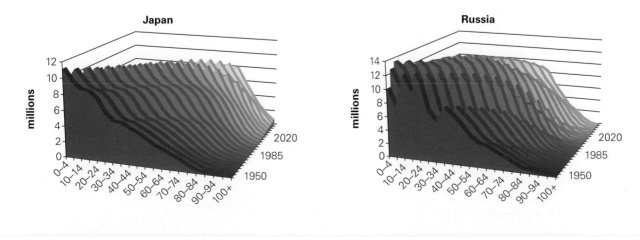

2.3 Demographic Change, 1950–2050, by Five-Year Age Group—continued

India's population will also age, albeit less than China's.

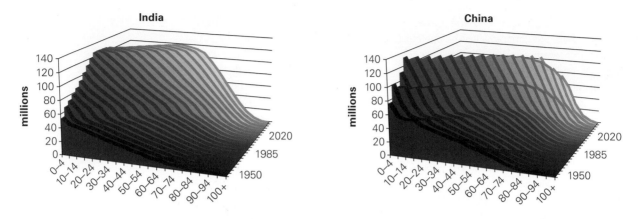

Latin America's population will age, and Africa's shows the devastating effects of HIV/ AIDS on longevity.

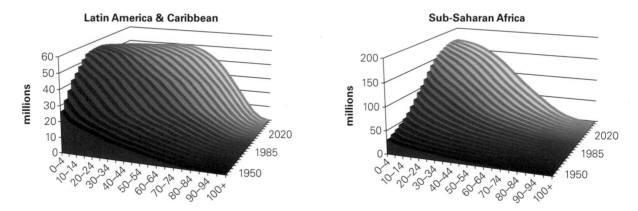

Source: Population Division of the Department of Economic and Social Affairs of the United Nations Secretariat. 2005 and 2006. "World Population Prospects: The 2006 Revision" and "World Urbanization Prospects: The 2005 Revision." Available at: http://esa.un.org/unpp.

2.4 Urban Population and Urbanization Rate, 1960–2006

Both as a result of population growth within urban areas and in-migration from rural areas, the world is becoming increasingly urbanized. A threshold was crossed in 2008: 50 percent of the world population is now urban. There is a lot more urbanization to come, as countries industrialize and grow.

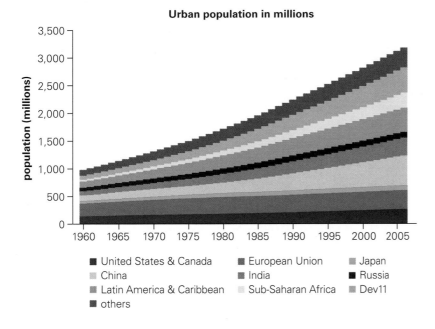

Urban population in millions

- United States & Canada
- European Union
- Japan
- China
- India
- Russia
- Latin America & Caribbean
- Sub-Saharan Africa
- Dev11
- others

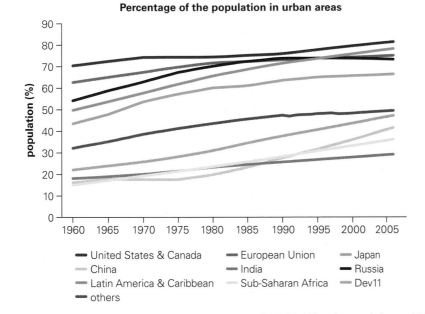

Percentage of the population in urban areas

- United States & Canada
- European Union
- Japan
- China
- India
- Russia
- Latin America & Caribbean
- Sub-Saharan Africa
- Dev11
- others

Sources: United Nations World Urbanization Prospects; World Bank, World Development Indicators 2007.

2.5 Population Growth to 2030: Low- and Middle-Income versus High-Income Countries

Most of the increase in population in the next two decades will take place in the cities of today's developing countries.

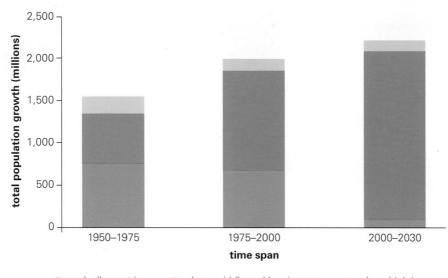

Legend: ■ rural, all countries   ■ urban, middle and low income   ■ urban, high income

Source: United Nations World Urbanization Prospects.

2.6 Female Labor Force and Female Participation Rate, 1980 to Present

The participation of women in the labor force has increased in industrialized countries and in Latin America and the Dev11, but participation rates have declined in India, China, and Russia. The reasons behind these declining trends have not been studied and are poorly understood. Declining trends may be explained by the upward trends in school enrollment, to the extent that participation in labor comes from girls who should otherwise be enrolled. Another possible explanation is inelastic labor demand for women for a variety of sociological and cultural reasons. The conclusion is that more work is needed to understand the meaning of these data and whether data collection captures informal work by women. Additionally, some of these trends should be disaggregated by age and education, and labor market issues in general should be looked at more deeply.

Another issue with data on female participation in the labor force is comparability across countries. In general, estimates of women in the labor force are lower than those of men and are not comparable internationally, reflecting the fact that for women, demographic, social, legal, and cultural trends and norms determine whether their activities are regarded as economic. In many countries large numbers of women work on farms or in other family enterprises without pay, while others work in or near their homes, mixing work and family activities during the day. Countries differ in the criteria used to determine whether such workers are to be counted as part of the labor force.

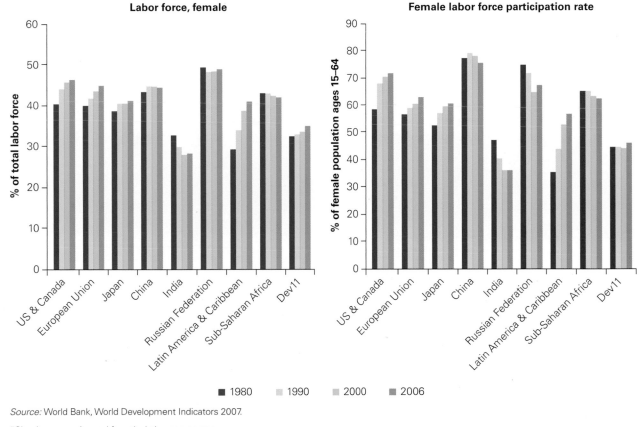

Source: World Bank, World Development Indicators 2007.

*Simple average is used for calculating aggregates.

3. POVERTY

3.1 Number of People Living below US$2 a Day and Percentage in Population

Reduction of poverty has been an explicit or implicit goal of governments in many developing countries since at least the end of WWII. India has pioneered the formulation of poverty concepts and measurements since the 1950s, including the use of household surveys, and is the developing country with the longest consistent series of poverty indicators. Starting in the 1990s, the World Bank built on this and other developing countries' measurement efforts. It supported the design and implementation of household surveys in a large number of countries and popularized a number of methodologies, concepts, and measurements.

These efforts helped develop poverty lines that allow comparisons across countries and over time. Poverty definitions vary from country to country. In some countries, the poor are defined as those in the lowest quintile or the lowest third of the income distribution. As a result, the number of poor never declines. A reduction in poverty in this context means an improvement in the incomes of those at the bottom of the distribution. In other countries, the poor are those who consume below a certain level considered minimal. The definition of "minimal" varies of course from country to country, depending on their level of development, incomes, values, and norms: what is considered essential in one country may be part of what is superfluous in another. A common definition applicable across countries addresses this problem and allows countries to be compared with each other.

This is what the poverty line valued at US$1 or US$2 achieves. It uses as a poverty line a common basket of commodities valued at common prices or purchasing power parities (PPPs). By this definition, while the number of poor has remained relatively stable since the early 1990s, the number of poor as a proportion of the total population has declined because the total population in developing countries has increased.

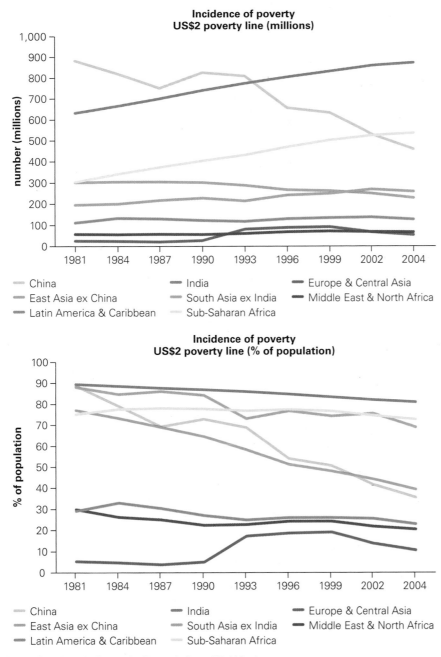

**Incidence of poverty
US$2 poverty line (millions)**

number (millions)

— China
— East Asia ex China
— Latin America & Caribbean

— India
— South Asia ex India
— Sub-Saharan Africa

— Europe & Central Asia
— Middle East & North Africa

**Incidence of poverty
US$2 poverty line (% of population)**

% of population

— China
— East Asia ex China
— Latin America & Caribbean

— India
— South Asia ex India
— Sub-Saharan Africa

— Europe & Central Asia
— Middle East & North Africa

Source: Development Economics Research Group, World Bank.

3.2 Gini Coefficients: Selected Examples

Poverty incidence measures provide information on the number of people consuming less than what is considered nutritionally and socially desirable. Although they are the most telling measure of a country's economic and social performance, there exist more subtle measures. Often the Gini coefficient is used: it calculates the distance from an absolutely equal income distribution among citizens, which is when the Gini coefficient would be equal to zero. Conversely, the more unequal the distribution, the closer to 1 is the Gini coefficient. In the most extreme case in which one citizen has all of the GDP and the rest of the population zero, the coefficient would be equal to 1.

The table below highlights some regional differences. Latin American countries—in particular Brazil and Chile—have much more unequal distribution of income than in Asia. Tanzania is an interesting exception in a region where income distribution tends to be as unequal as in Latin America. This is possibly the result of the land reform programs under President Nyerere.

The actual calculation of Gini coefficients is complex and requires income data at the household level that often do not exist. The distribution of expenditure at the household level is used instead in these cases, which often tends to bias results toward more equality than really exists. The periodicity of the data is another issue. In most countries, income or expenditure distribution data are available at infrequently intervals only. Comparisons between countries and over time should hence be made carefully. For example, the map that follows shows the United States with a more equal distribution than China's. But the coefficient for China is calculated on the basis of 2004 data, and that of the United States on the basis of 2000 data, and most observers would agree that coefficients in the two countries now are believed to be quite close to each other—in the mid 40s.

The table below also provides some information on the evolution of the distribution of income in selected countries. It shows that income distribution has worsened in Bangladesh, China, and India, countries that have experienced rapid growth in the last two decades. In Brazil, where per capita income has stagnated over the last 25 years, income distribution improved as a result of the end of hyperinflation (which penalized the poor disproportionately) and the implementation of redistributive programs. In Chile, Indonesia, and Morocco, the income distribution has remained relatively stable.

Gini Coefficients of Selected Countries (times 100)

Country	Year 1	Year 2	Gini in year 1	Gini in year 2
Bangladesh	1991–92	2005	28.27	33.20
Brazil	1990	2004	60.68	56.99
Chile	1990	2003	55.52	54.92
China	1990	2004	33.50	46.90
India	1993–94	2004–05	31.52	36.76
Indonesia	1993	2004	34.63	34.76
Morocco	1990–91	1998–99	39.20	39.46
Tanzania	1991	2000–01	33.83	34.62

Source: World Bank, World Development Indicators 2007.

3.3 Gini Coefficients around the World

The map below provides a more thorough picture of Gini coefficients and highlights that equity has regional dimensions. Inequality is high in many South American countries: Brazil is not unique. Tanzania, with a Gini coefficient closer to Asia's values, is an exception in a continent where income inequality is extremely high.

Gini Coefficients from the UN Human Development Report, 2007–2008

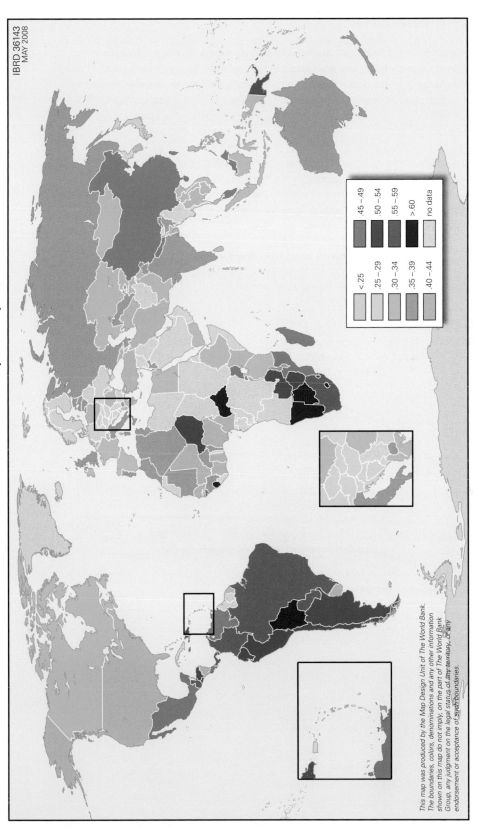

IBRD 36143
MAY 2008

<.25		45 – .49	
.25 – .29		.50 – .54	
.30 – .34		.55 – .59	
.35 – .39		>.60	
.40 – .44		no data	

This map was produced by the Map Design Unit of The World Bank. The boundaries, colors, denominations and any other information shown on this map do not imply, on the part of The World Bank Group, any judgment on the legal status of any territory, or any endorsement or acceptance of such boundaries.

3.4 Growth Incidence Curves

Growth incidence curves help illustrate the evolution of income distribution by calculating the rate of income growth for each household. When high-income groups see their incomes rise faster than the bottom group, income distribution worsens, even though the whole population sees an increase in incomes.

3.4.1 China

The growth incidence curve for China between 1993 and 2004 illustrates this point. During this period, the annual per capita growth rate was close to 7 percent per year. For the top half of the population in terms of income the increase was above 7 percent, and for the bottom half it was below. The highest income groups benefited more, probably because their skills and assets were in shorter supply.

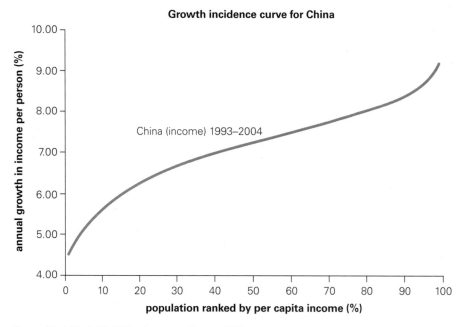

Growth incidence curve for China

China (income) 1993–2004

Source: World Bank, World Development Indicators 2007.

Note: Per capita income has been adjusted by the cost of living difference between the rural and urban areas.

3.4.2 India

The case of India is more difficult to interpret. Whereas national accounts data indicate that per capita income between 1993 and 2004 increased in excess of 4 percent per year, household surveys show dramatically smaller increases in consumption expenditure—implausibly smaller. The reasons for the discrepancy have been the subject of considerable debate in India. But India is not unique in this aspect. Already in 1999, Angus Deaton* had observed that in many countries discrepancies between household surveys and national accounts were a serious issue deserving serious investigation. This suggestion unfortunately has not been followed up, and one of the many statistical shortcomings in developing countries persists.

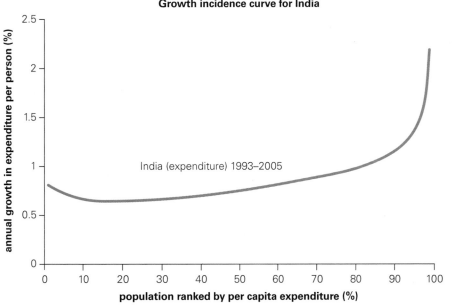

Growth incidence curve for India

India (expenditure) 1993–2005

Source: World Bank, World Development Indicators 2007.

Note: Per capita consumption expenditure has been adjusted by the cost of living difference between the rural and urban areas.

*Deaton, Angus. 1999. "Saving and Growth." In Luis Serven and Klaus Schmitt-Hebbel, *Economics of Savings and Growth*. Cambridge, UK: Cambridge University Press.

3.5 Ratios of Quintile Shares, Selected Countries

Tracking each population quintile's consumption as a share of GDP is another way of capturing the extent of inequality. In the case of Brazil, the richest 20 percent of the population had more than half of the country's income, whereas in India the top quintile had between one third and 40 percent of income, and in China between 40 and 45 percent. The ratio between top and bottom quintile consumption is another measure of inequality: it varies between a high of more than 20:1 in Brazil, to less than 10:1 in China, to much less in India or Bangladesh.

Country	Year 1	Year 2	Quintile share					
			Bottom in year1	Top in year1	Bottom in year 2	Top in year 2	Top/bottom in yr 1	Top/bottom in yr 2
Bangladesh	1991–92	2005	9.4	33.9	8.8	37.6	3.6	4.3
Brazil	1990	2004	2.3	55.7	2.6	53.0	23.9	20.2
Chile	1990	2003	3.4	52.8	3.7	52.7	15.4	14.3
China	1990	2004	5.6	41.5	4.3	44.5	7.4	10.5
India	1993–94	2004–05	8.9	36.3	8.1	40.4	4.1	5.0
Indonesia	1993	2004	8.3	38.0	8.0	38.0	4.6	4.8
Morocco	1990–91	1998–99	6.6	40.9	6.4	40.7	6.2	6.3
Tanzania	1991	2000–01	7.4	36.8	7.3	37.2	5.0	5.1

Source: World Bank, World Development Indicators 2007.

3.6 Inequality over Time: Annual Change in Gini Coefficient in 59 Developing Countries

Over the last decade, it has become increasingly clear that inequality is rising in many countries, including industrialized ones. The IMF World Economic Outlook documented this trend in its most recent 2008 report. The figure below shows that inequality has increased in most countries. The reasons are not entirely well understood. In industrialized countries, inequality may result from the integration of China and India into the global economy, which puts pressure on low and unskilled labor, technological progress, and migration. Which of these factors matters most is the subject of considerable debate and controversy. In developing countries on a high growth path, the rise in income inequality seems to be the consequence of the movement of people from low- to high-productivity activities and sectors.

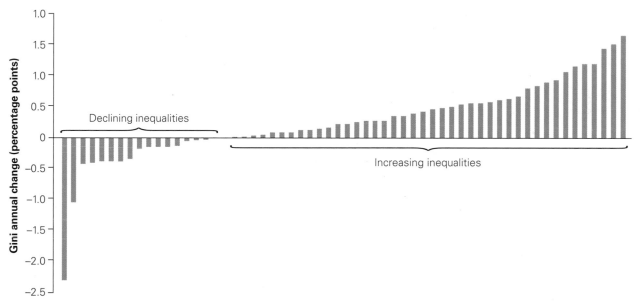

Source: World Bank, Global Monitoring Report 2008.

Note: The time period varies depending on the availability of data. Typically it is from late 1980s and early 1990s to later 1990s and early 2000s.

4. SOCIOECONOMIC INDICATORS

4.1 Improved Sanitation Facilities and Water Source, 1990–2004

Developing countries lag behind industrialized countries in terms of access to infrastructure and other services that are crucial determinants of health outcomes. It is well-known, for example, that frequently malnutrition develops not from insufficient intake of food, but from diseases associated with lack of access to sanitation and potable water.

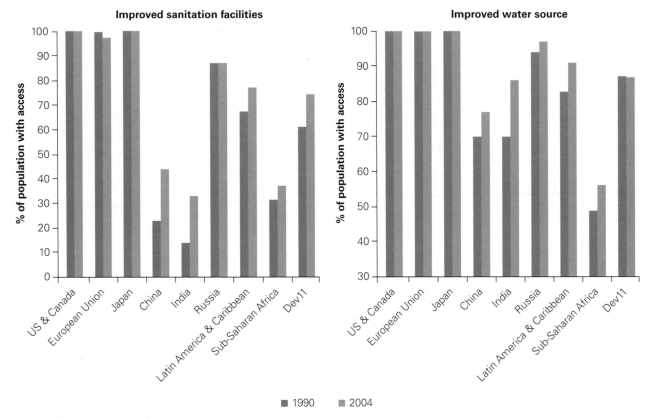

Source: World Bank, World Development Indicators 2007.

Improved sanitation facilities: Access to improved sanitation facilities refers to the percentage of the population with at least adequate access to excreta disposal facilities that can effectively prevent human, animal, and insect contact with excreta. Improved facilities range from simple but protected pit latrines to flush toilets with a sewerage connection. To be effective, facilities must be correctly constructed and properly maintained. See World Health Organization and United Nations Children's Fund, Meeting the MDG Drinking Water and Sanitation Target, for details.

Improved water source: Access to an improved water source refers to the percentage of the population with reasonable access to an adequate amount of water from an improved source, such as a household connection, public standpipe, borehole, protected well or spring, and rainwater collection. Unimproved sources include vendors, tanker trucks, and unprotected wells and springs. Reasonable access is defined as the availability of at least 20 liters a person a day from a source within one kilometer of the dwelling. See World Health Organization and United Nations Children's Fund, Meeting the MDG Drinking Water and Sanitation Target, for details.

4.2 DPT* and Measles Immunization, 1995–2005

Although there has been considerable improvement, access to the most basic public good, vaccines, remains remarkably uneven.

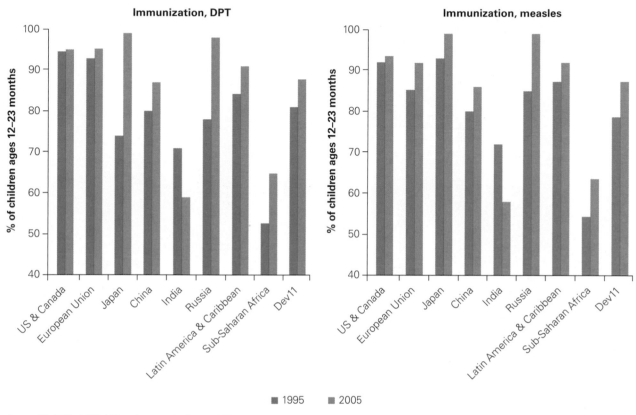

■ 1995   ■ 2005

Source: World Bank, World Development Indicators 2007.

*Diphtheria, pertussis (or whooping cough), and tetanus.

4.3 Prevalence of Undernourishment* and HIV/AIDS

Although there have been improvements everywhere except in Sub-Saharan Africa, undernourishment and HIV remain serious health problems in developing countries, even in the rapidly growing ones.

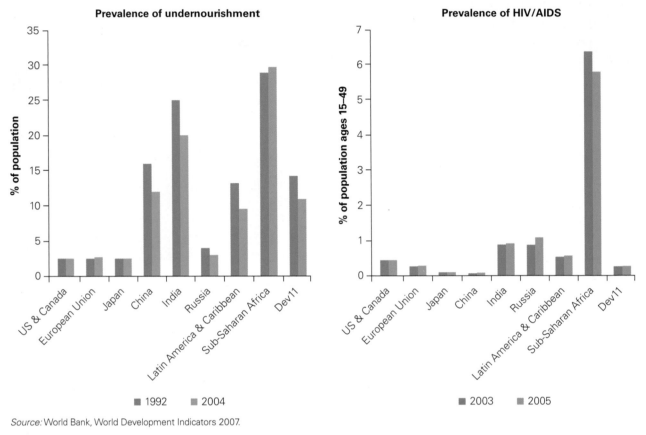

Prevalence of undernourishment

Prevalence of HIV/AIDS

■ 1992 ■ 2004

■ 2003 ■ 2005

Source: World Bank, World Development Indicators 2007.

*Population below minimum level of dietary energy consumption.

4.4 Public Spending on Education (2004)* and Expected Years of Schooling (2005)**

It is extremely hard to compile statistics on education that make sense. For example, years of schooling is a function of both public and private spending on education, but data on private spending are not collected systematically.

Another problem is that in most countries, public spending in education is done mostly by the lower levels of government—provincial and city governments—but these data are not systematically collected and processed, with the result that public spending on education is typically underestimated.

Last but not least, years of schooling is a poor proxy to learning achievements, which is the real output of any school system. But developing better data on this will take years of effort.

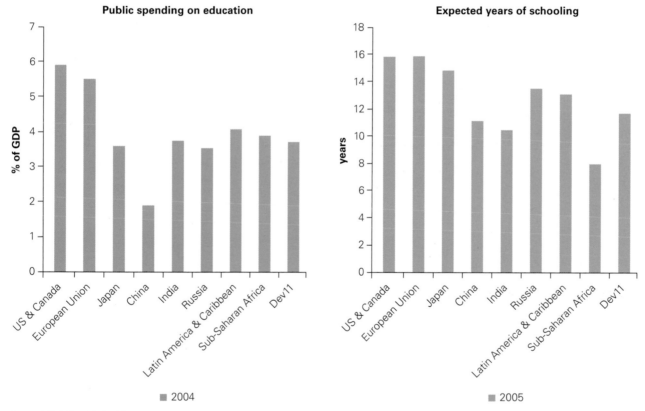

Source: World Bank, World Development Indicators 2007.

*Most recent year (1999) is used for China.

**The number of years a child of school entrance age is expected to spend at school or university, including years spent on repetition.

4.5 Primary School Enrollment* and Completion Rate

The statistics that are collected suggest that in most countries primary enrollment and
completion rates have increased and are getting closer to industrialized levels, except for
Africa and India, where they remain at lower levels.

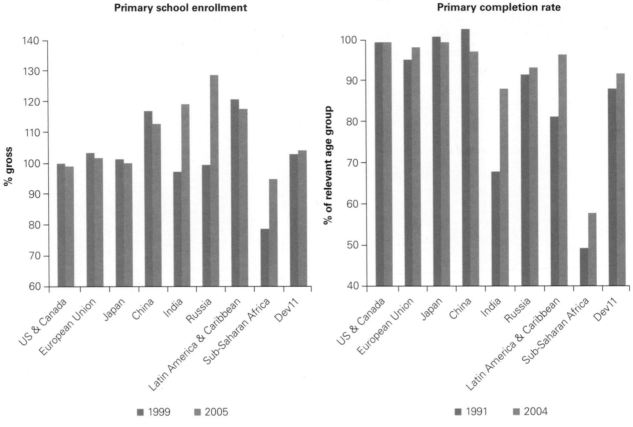

Primary school enrollment

Primary completion rate

1999   2005

1991   2004

Source: World Bank, World Development Indicators 2007.

*Ratio of total enrollment, regardless of age, to the population of the age group that officially corresponds to the level of education shown.

4.6 Adult and Youth Literacy Rates

Low enrollment rates generally translate into low literacy rates among adults and young people.

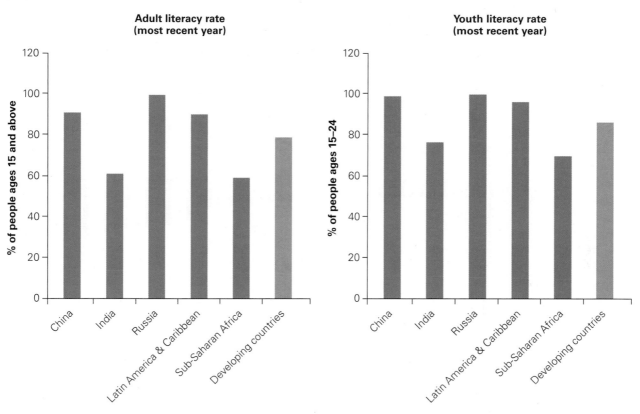

Adult literacy rate (most recent year)

Youth literacy rate (most recent year)

Source: World Bank, World Development Indicators 2007.

4.7 PISA Tests: 2006

Learning achievements—that is the acquisition of specific cognitive skills—when they are measured, are quite varied both within and across countries. The so-called PISA tests consist of elaborate evaluations meant to determine the learning achievements of students in science. The results show significant variance between and within countries.

Percentage of students at each proficiency level on the science scale

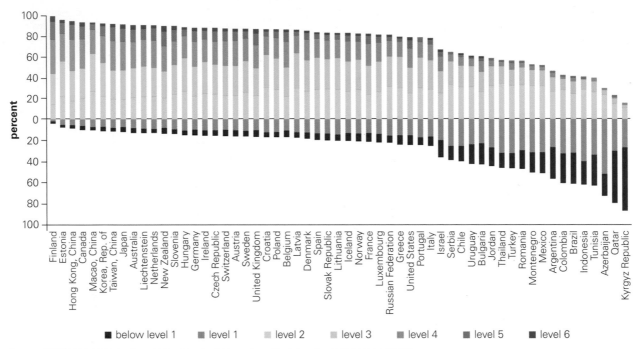

legend: ■ below level 1 ■ level 1 ■ level 2 ■ level 3 ■ level 4 ■ level 5 ■ level 6

Source: OECD PISA 2006 database, Table 2.1a. Available at: http://dx.doi.org/10.1787/141844475532

Note: Countries are ranked in descending order of percentage of 15-year-old at Levels 2, 3, 4, 5, and 6. Above the zero line one finds the proportion of students in the country that has higher ratings than level 1. Below the zero line, one finds the proportion of students with level 1 and below.

5. INFRASTRUCTURE

Investment in infrastructure is key for growth and development because it expands the range of opportunities for and returns on private investment. Furthermore, investment in infrastructure ensures access to key public services such as water, public transportation, and urban amenities—services that not only support growth but also and in turn help distribute the benefits of growth across the population at large. Given the importance of infrastructure for long-term growth and inclusiveness, available data are surprisingly hard to obtain. There appear to be two main reasons for this. First, public investment is generally carried out by various levels of government and agencies whose expenditures are not part of the budget. Very few countries consolidate these various sources of infrastructure spending in their national accounts. Second, private investment in infrastructure is rarely fully recorded. India is an exception in both these dimensions; but for other countries, the information base needs to be built.

5.1 Infrastructure Investment

Infrastructure Investment in Major Latin American Countries (% of GDP)

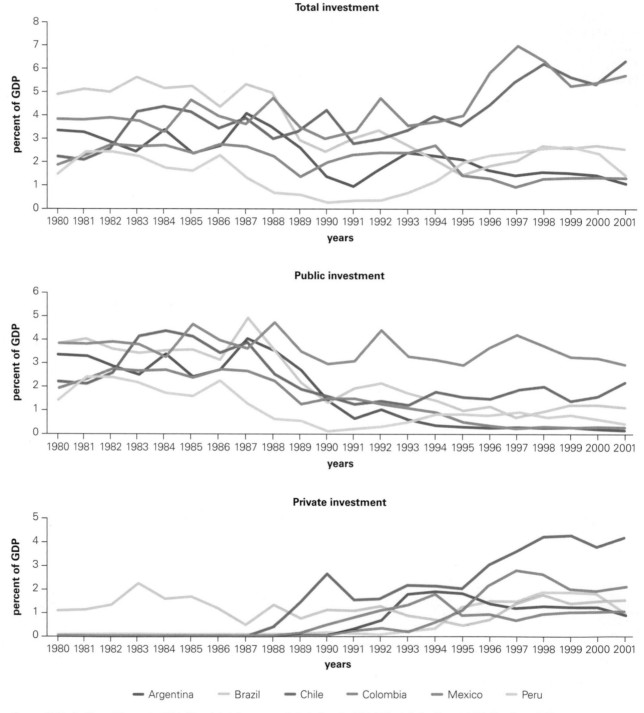

Source: Calderón, C., and Serven, L. 2004. "Trends in Infrastructure in Latin America." World Bank Policy Research Working Paper 3401.

Brazil: Primary Deficit and Public Infrastructure Investment (% of GDP)

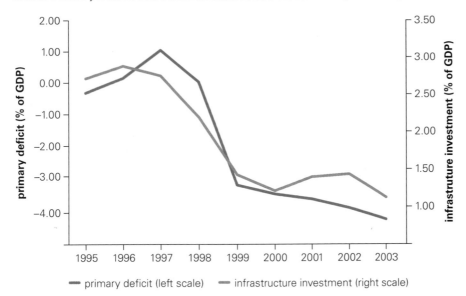

— primary deficit (left scale) — infrastructure investment (right scale)

Source: Afonso, J., et al. 2005. "Fiscal Space and Public Sector Investments in Infrastructure: A Brazilian Case Study." IPEA Texto para Discussao 1141.

India: Gross Domestic Capital Formation in Infrastructure Sectors (% of GDP)

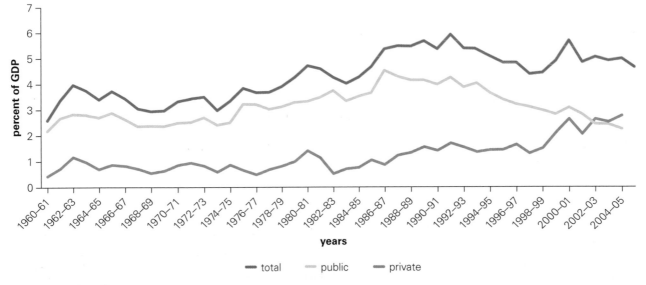

— total — public — private

Source: Government of India data.

Pakistan: Infrastructure Investment (% of GDP)

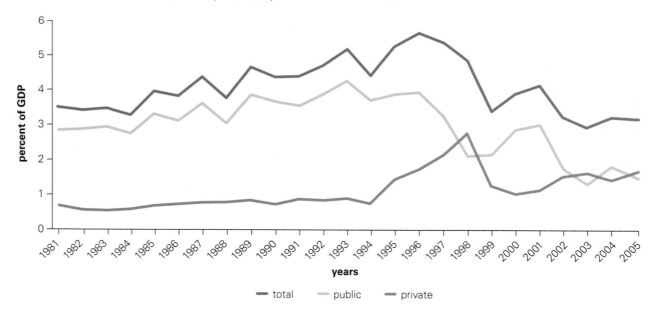

South Africa: Infrastructure Investment (% of GDP)

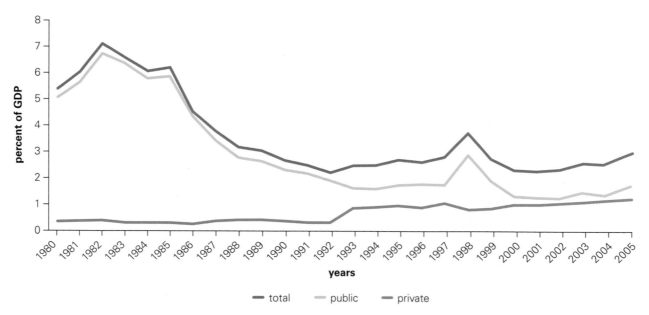

The Growth Report: Strategies for Sustained Growth and Inclusive Development

Turkey: Infrastructure Investment (% of GDP)

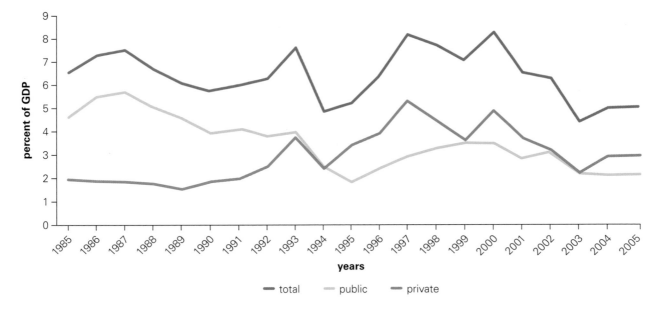

years

— total   — public   — private

Thailand: Infrastructure Investment (% of GDP)

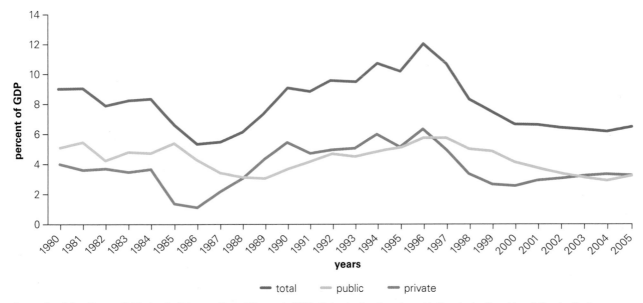

years

— total   — public   — private

Source: for all four figures, Calderón, C., Odawara, R., and Serven, L. 2008. "Infrastructure Investment in Developing Countries: A Quarter-Century Retrospective." Mimeo, World Bank.

6. GLOBAL TRENDS

The post WWII period was characterized by a number of important global trends, some of which represent a clear break with the past and a change in direction.

6.1 Inflation*

The last 20 years saw a decline in the rate of inflation. The decline started in industrialized countries and was followed after a lag by developing countries.

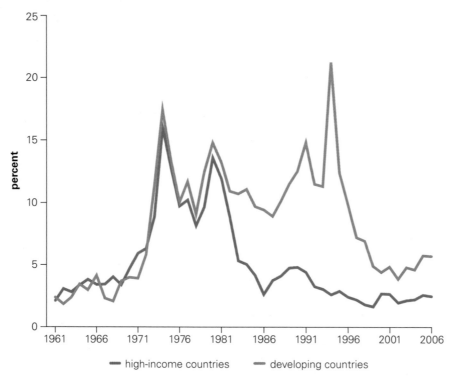

Source: World Bank, World Development Indicators 2007.

*Inflation is measured by the median inflation rate in both groups of countries.

6.2 Real Interest Rate,* 1960–2005

Domestic real interest rates increased significantly, because in most developing countries, nominal rates declined less than the decline in inflation.

Source: World Bank, World Development Indicators 2007.

*Real interest rates are measured by the median inflation rate in both groups of countries.

6.3 Emerging Markets Risk Spreads,* 2000–08

Risks spreads for emerging markets have substantially declined in the last eight years because of fiscal consolidation, improved debt management, and buildup of reserves.

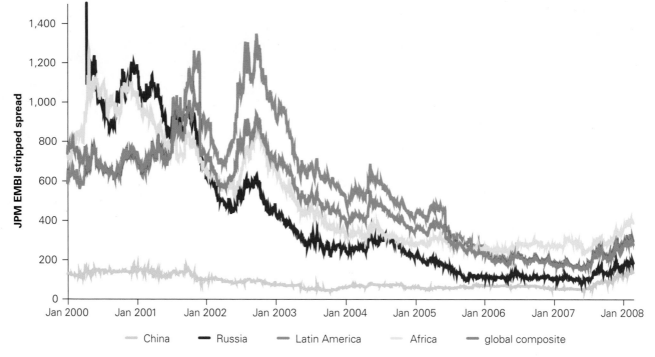

Source: JP Morgan Government Bond Indices.

*In the calculation of JP Morgan EMBI Stripped Spreads, the value of collateralized flows (if any) is stripped from the bond and hence it provides a better measure of the credit risk premium over United States Treasury bonds.

6.4 Commodity Prices

The third important development, more recent than the previous two, is a return to higher commodity prices. This has been felt in all classes of commodities, as shown in the next four graphs. Agriculture and food indices rose markedly less than other commodities but they have been catching up in recent months.

6.4.1 World Bank Major Commodity Price Indices*

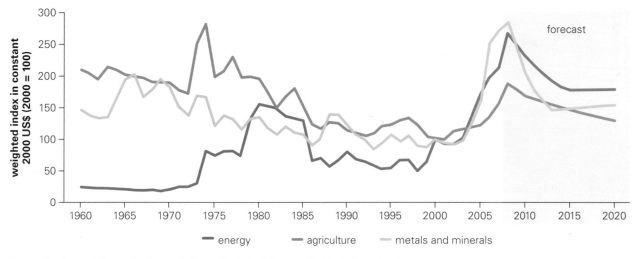

Source: Development Economics Prospects Group, World Bank, Commodity Price Data: various issues.

*World Bank commodity price indices are trade-weighted indices for developing countries.

6.4.2 Selected Metals Prices*

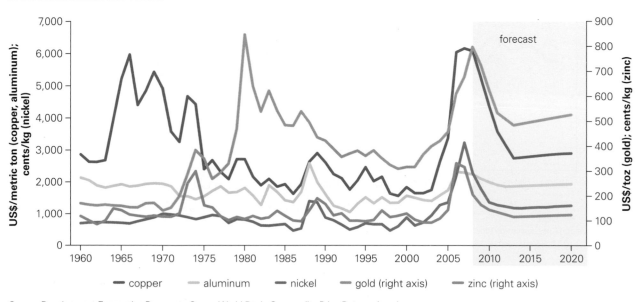

Source: Development Economics Prospects Group, World Bank, Commodity Price Data: various issues.

*Real metal price in constant 1990 US$.

6.4.3 Agriculture: Indices for Various Categories of Products

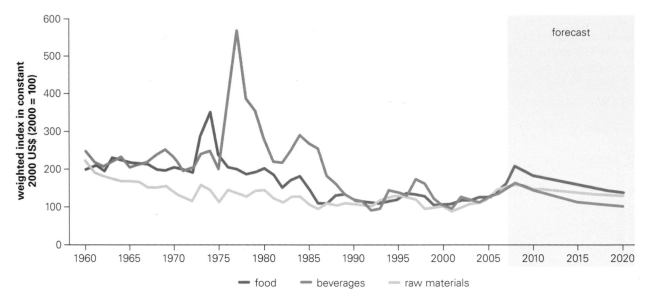

Source: Development Economics Prospects Group, World Bank, Commodity Price Data: various issues.

6.4.4 Food: Indices for Various Categories of Products

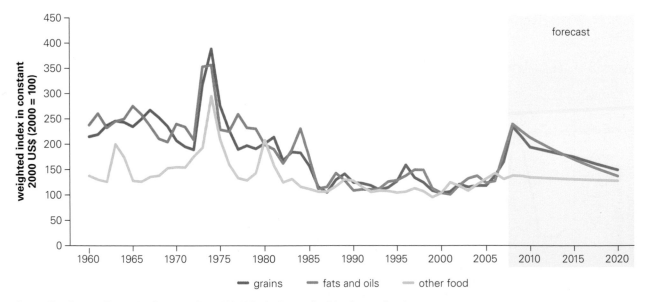

Source: Development Economics Prospects Group, World Bank, Commodity Price Data: various issues.

6.5 Global Savings Rates* for Developed and Developing Countries as Percent of GDP

Saving rates have been declining in industrialized countries and increasing in developing countries. During the last decade, developing countries have become net exporters of capital.

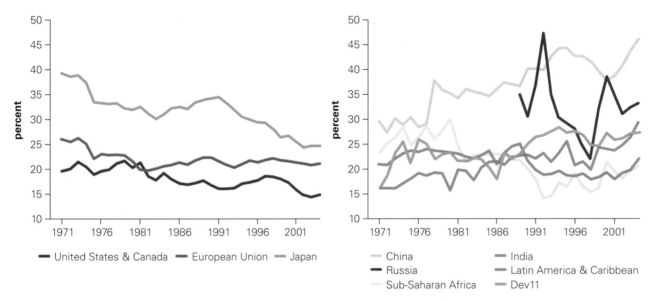

Source: World Bank, World Development Indicators 2007.

*Gross domestic savings rates are gross domestic savings (GDP less final consumption expenditure (total consumption)) as percentage of GDP, both in current US$.

6.6 Global Investment Rates* for Developed and Developing Countries as Percent of GDP

Investment rates have followed movements in saving rates—that is, declining in industrialized countries and rising in most developing countries. The exceptions are Sub-Saharan Africa and Latin America, where rates of investment and growth have been stagnant.

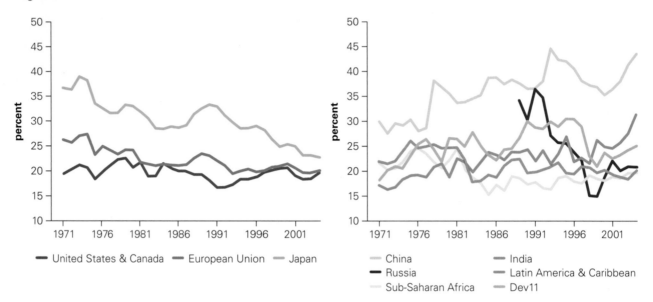

— United States & Canada — European Union — Japan

— China — India
— Russia — Latin America & Caribbean
— Sub-Saharan Africa — Dev11

Source: World Bank, World Development Indicators 2007.

*Gross domestic investment rates are gross capital formation (formerly gross domestic investment, which consists of outlays on additions to the fixed assets of the economy plus net changes in the level of inventories) as percentage of GDP, both in current US$.

6.7 Size of Government (government expenditure as share of GDP) of Developed and Developing Countries, 1960–2005

The size of government is another important macroeconomic variable that is difficult to estimate precisely because some government expenditure and investment takes place in public enterprises. These are not always consolidated into the government accounts. This leads to variability, and a tendency to understate the figures.

Government consumption expenditure

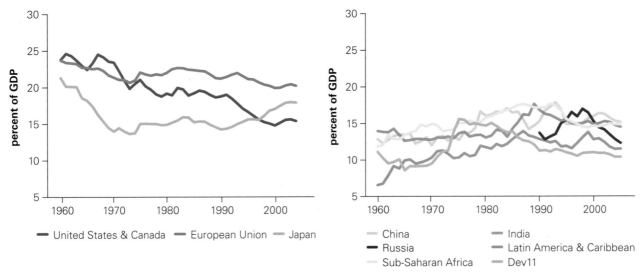

Source: World Bank, World Development Indicators 2007.

Note: Government expenditure includes all government spending in goods and services, for consumption and investment, and net lending.

General government total expenditure and net lending

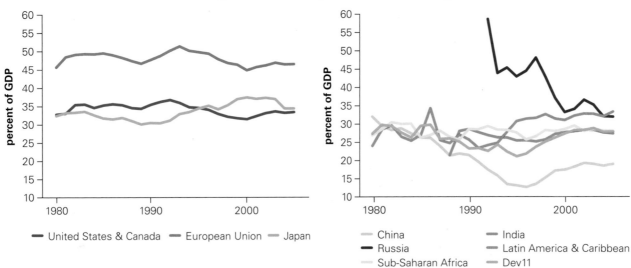

Source: IMF, World Economic Outlook.

6.8 International Trade

Since WWII, international trade has grown faster than global GDP. This is illustrated in the three graphs below.

6.8.1 Evolution of World Exports and the Share of Developing Countries, 1975–2005

World exports grew from less than 20 percent of global GDP in 1975 to 30 percent in 2005. The share of developing countries in global exports increased from about 22 percent to about 28 percent. The increase came after a sharp decline in the mid-1980s when the oil price dropped to about US$10/bbl by about 1986. In constant United States dollar terms, the share of developing countries' exports appear more stable.

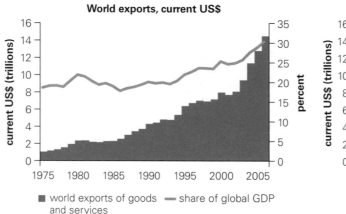

World exports, current US$

■ world exports of goods and services — share of global GDP

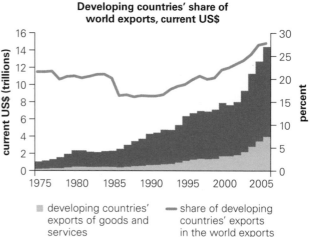

Developing countries' share of world exports, current US$

■ developing countries' exports of goods and services — share of developing countries' exports in the world exports

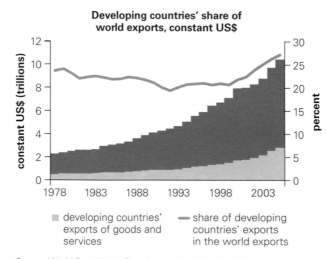

Developing countries' share of world exports, constant US$

■ developing countries' exports of goods and services — share of developing countries' exports in the world exports

Source: World Bank, World Development Indicators 2007.

6.8.2 Developing Countries' Exports of Manufactures and Commodities*

The growth in exports of developing countries comes from both manufactures and commodities. The figures below show exports measured in nominal United States dollars and hence include price effects.

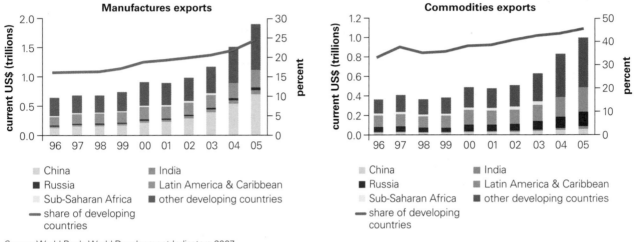

Source: World Bank, World Development Indicators 2007.

*Estimates for Sub-Saharan Africa not available in 2004 and 2005; for all trade data, regional aggregates do not exclude intraregional trade.

6.8.3 More Export Opportunities for High-Income Countries and South-South Trade, 1980–2005

Two new trends emerged in the 1990s: developing countries' imports grew faster than industrialized countries' exports, and developing countries' exports grew faster than industrialized countries' imports. The first trend indicates that developing countries' markets are increasingly open to industrialized countries. Both trends suggest increasing South-South trade (see the figures below).

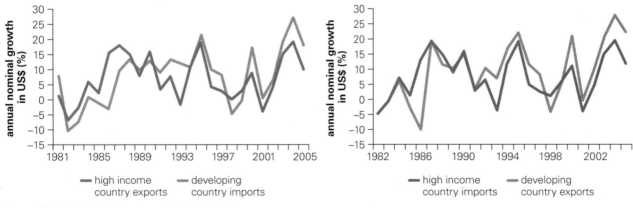

Source: World Bank, World Development Indicators 2007.

6.9 Global Migration and Remittances

Since World War II, migration has become an increasingly important component of development. The number of immigrants has more than tripled, and remittances have been growing as a share of developing countries' GDP.

6.9.1 Global Migration and Remittances, 1960 to 2005

The number of immigrants has more than tripled. As a proportion of the world population, migration has increased from about 2.5 percent to 3 percent, and probably much more as a proportion of industrialized countries' population. Not surprisingly, remittances have become an increasingly large share of developing countries' GDP.

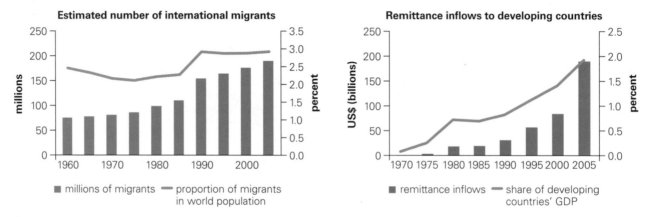

Source: Population Division, United Nations, "Trends in Total Migrant Stock: 2005 Revision"; World Bank staff estimates based on the International Monetary Fund's *Balance of Payments Statistics Yearbook 2007.*

6.9.2 Remittances in Relation to FDI and Aid, 1970 to 2005

Remittances now exceed official development assistance.

Source: World Bank staff estimates based on the International Monetary Fund's *Balance of Payments Statistics Yearbook 2007;* World Bank, *World Development Indicators* and *Global Development Finance,* 2007; International Monetary Fund, International Financial Statistics and Balance of Payments databases.

6.10 Role of Technological Advances in Developing Countries' Economies

Developing countries have become technologically more sophisticated, as indicated in the graphs below.

6.10.1 Share of Developing Countries' High-Technology* Exports and Detailed Decomposition

Developing countries' share of high-technology exports has been increasing rapidly in recent years, driven mostly by China, but also other Asian countries.

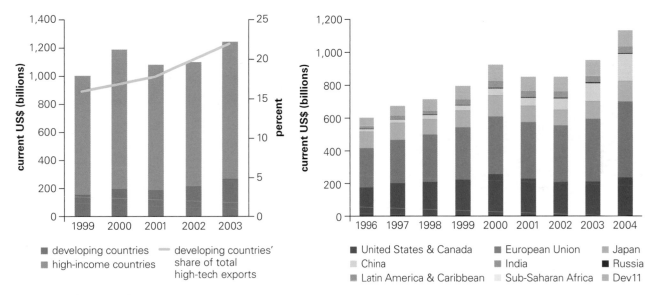

Source: World Bank, World Development Indicators 2007.

Note: For all trade data, regional aggregates do not exclude intraregional trade.

*High-technology exports are products with high R&D intensity, such as in aerospace, computers, pharmaceuticals, scientific instruments, and electrical machinery.

6.10.2 Exports of Knowledge-Based* Commercial Services Dominated by the United States and the European Union

In the case of services, world trade is still dominated by the United States and the European Union. Notwithstanding India's growing exports of services, the share of developing countries has in fact declined.

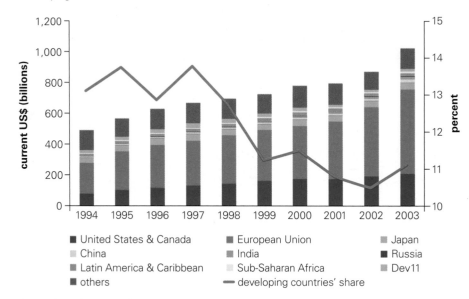

Source: World Bank, World Development Indicators 2007.

*Knowledge-based commercial services include information technology (IT), communications, insurance, financial, and other services; but do not include transportation and travel. Typical activities are international telecommunications and postal and courier services; computer data processing; news-related service transactions between residents and nonresidents; construction services; royalties and license fees; miscellaneous business, professional, and technical services; personal, cultural, and recreational services; freight insurance on goods exported and other direct insurance such as life insurance; financial intermediation services such as commissions, foreign exchange transactions, and brokerage services; and auxiliary services such as financial market operational and regulatory services.

6.10.3 Developing Countries' Share of Patent Applications (residents and nonresidents), 1995–2004

Developing countries have become more important innovators.

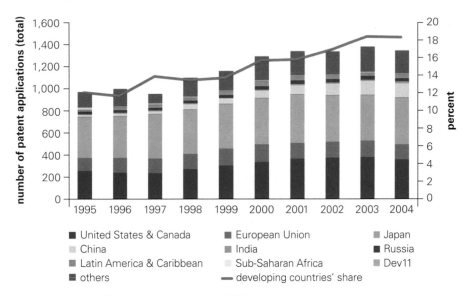

- United States & Canada
- European Union
- Japan
- China
- India
- Russia
- Latin America & Caribbean
- Sub-Saharan Africa
- Dev11
- others
- — developing countries' share

Source: World Bank, World Development Indicators 2007.

6.10.4 Receipts of Royalty and License Fees, 1997–2004

However, income from innovation is still dominated by industrialized countries.

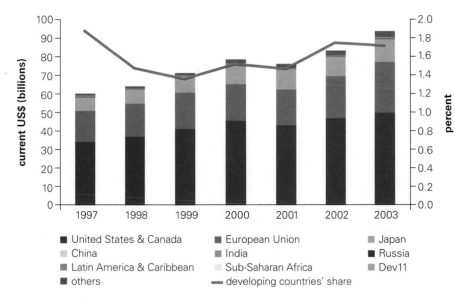

- United States & Canada
- European Union
- Japan
- China
- India
- Russia
- Latin America & Caribbean
- Sub-Saharan Africa
- Dev11
- others
- — developing countries' share

Source: World Bank, World Development Indicators 2007.

6.11 Private Capital Flows to Developing Countries

Since the mid-1990s, private capital flows to developing countries have declined and developing countries now are net savers. The exception is FDI, whose role in recent years has increased, in both absolute and relative terms. This is illustrated in the figures below.

6.11.1 FDI Inflows to Developing Countries, 1980–2005

The inflows of FDI to developing countries are highly concentrated, with Latin America and China being the major recipients in the last 10 years. In aggregate terms, FDI to developing countries has been volatile. Between the mid-1990s and the early 2000s, inflows declined from 35 percent of total world FDI to 10 percent. FDI inflows have now recovered and are hovering around 30 percent of the world total.

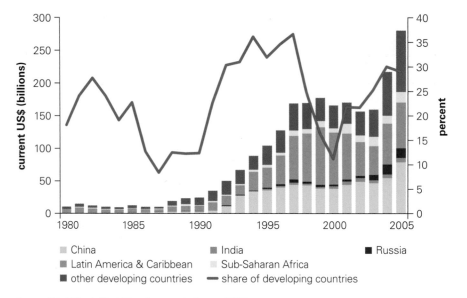

Source: World Bank, World Development Indicators 2007.

6.11.2 Private Capital Flows* into Developing Countries and Their Share in Total Private Capital Flows, 1991–2005

After reaching over 25 percent of the world total in the early 1990s, private capital flows into developing countries are a small and declining portion of all private capital flows.

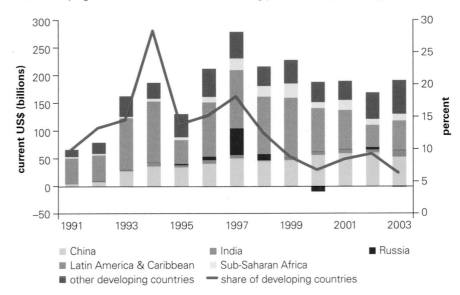

China
India
Russia
Latin America & Caribbean
Sub-Saharan Africa
other developing countries
share of developing countries

Source: World Bank, World Development Indicators 2007.

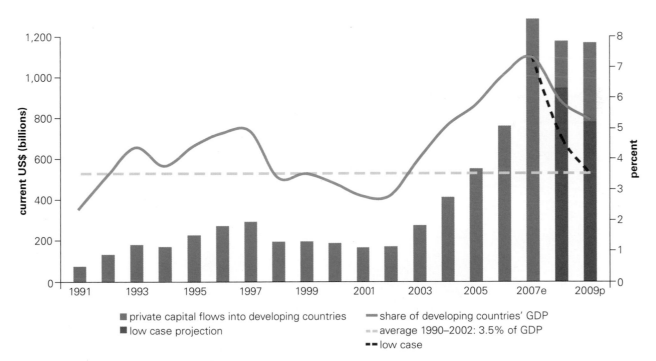

private capital flows into developing countries
low case projection
share of developing countries' GDP
average 1990–2002: 3.5% of GDP
low case

Source: World Bank, Development Economics Group.

*Private capital flows consist of private debt and nondebt flows. Private debt flows include commercial bank lending, bonds, and other private credits; nondebt private flows are FDI and portfolio equity investment.

6.11.3 Buildup of Reserves in Developing Countries, 1993–2006

Over the last decade, developing countries have started accumulating substantial reserves.

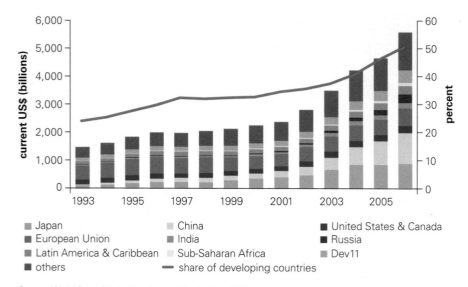

Source: World Bank, World Development Indicators 2007.

6.11.4 Global Imbalances, 1999–2006

The increase in developing economies' reserves occurred in parallel with a decline in the United States savings rate to unprecedentedly low levels.

	Global imbalance							
	1999	**2000**	**2001**	**2002**	**2003**	**2004**	**2005**	**2006**
Major reserve-positive economies								
Total reserves, top 10 (minus gold, current US$, millions)								
China	158	168	216	291	408	614	822	1068
Japan	287	355	395	461	663	834	834	880
Russian Federation	8	24	33	44	73	121	176	296
Taiwan, China	106	107	122	162	207	242	253	266
Korea, Rep. of	74	96	103	121	155	199	210	239
India	33	38	46	68	99	127	132	171
Singapore	77	80	76	82	96	113	116	136
Hong Kong, China	96	108	111	112	118	124	124	133
Brazil	35	32	36	38	49	53	54	86
Malaysia	31	28	30	33	44	66	70	82
U.S. household saving (current US$, billions)								
	114	117	108	169	166	160	13	6
As a percentage of household disposable income								
	1.7	1.6	1.4	2.2	2.0	1.8	0.1	0.1
U.S. current account deficit (current US$, billions)								
	300	415	389	472	528	665	729	857
Composition of U.S. capital inflows by major reserve holding economies (current US$, billions)								
Foreign-owned assets in the United States, excluding financial derivatives (increase/financial inflow (+))								
European Union	409	593	362	215	244	467	479	799
China	15	19	39	72	75	125	188	210
Middle East	2	16	2	1	8	28	19	63
Japan	25	58	50	77	139	238	61	48
Germany	49	72	62	18	40	35	32	42
Hong Kong, China	11	10	29	15	38	11	32	38
Brazil	−1	1	8	−2	10	3	10	32
Korea, Rep. of	11	1	1	14	18	19	22	16
Singapore	−2	9	0	8	11	12	5	
India	3	−1	0	3	7	−3	4	5
Taiwan, China	0	−2	9	11	23	8	11	4

Source: World Bank, World Development Indicators 2007; Bureau of Economic Analysis, National Economic Accounts Data and United States International Transactions Accounts Data.

6.12 Climate Change

Global warming and its potential costly consequences are a major, if not the most important, global trend facing developing economies. The figures below illustrate some of the magnitudes of the problem.

6.12.1 Per Capita Carbon Emission, 1970–2003

Per capita emissions of CO_2 are lower than those in industrialized countries, but rising rapidly.

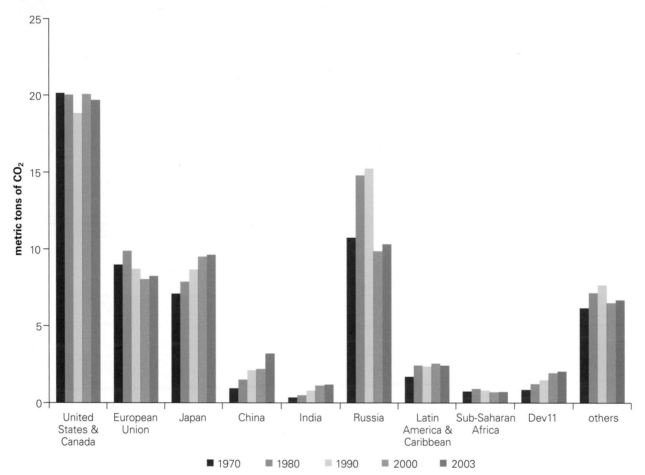

Source: World Bank, World Development Indicators 2007.

6.12.2 CO$_2$ Emissions in the United States, China, and India, Present and Future

Currently, China's total carbon emissions are approximately equal to those of the United States, and India's are about one fifth. On a per capita basis, however, India's emissions were 5 percent and China's 25 percent of United States levels. If India and China reduced emissions by 20 percent over the next 50 years (a period in which their per capita incomes are likely to grow to advanced-country levels) and the United States reduced emissions by 80 percent, then China and India's per capita emissions would be roughly equal and 20 percent of the United States levels, respectively.

Emissions in China and India as percentage of United States levels

	Total CO$_2$ emissions	Per capita emissions	Per capita GDP	Per capita emissions 80% reduction in United States and 20% in China and India
India (% of United States)	20	5	2	20
China (% of United States)	100	25	6	100

Source: UNDP, Human Development Report 2007.

6.12.3 Carbon Intensity in Selected Countries*

Industrialized countries produce much less CO$_2$ than developing countries per unit of output. This reflects more efficient technology, the production mix, and, possibly, energy costs, which tend to be more highly subsidized in developing countries.

Countries	Output
United States	0.46
European Union	0.29
Japan	0.19
China	1.67
India	1.30

Source: UNDP, Human Development Report 2007.

*Gigatons of CO$_2$ emissions per trillion United States dollars of GDP.

6.12.4 The Magnitude of the Challenge

The Intergovernmental Panel on Climate Change (IPCC) has assessed that a relatively safe level of CO_2 emissions globally is 14.5 gigatons per year, which comes out to 2.25 metric tons per person per year. The table below from the United Nations Human Development Report (2007) shows the per capita emissions for major industrial countries. World carbon emissions are now at about two times the safe level, meaning that if the current output is sustained, the CO_2 stock in the atmosphere will rise above safe levels in the next 40 years.

Global carbon footprints at OECD levels would require more than one planet[a]

	CO_2 emissions per capita (t CO_2) 2004	Equivalent global CO_2 emissions (Gt CO_2) 2004[b]	Equivalent number of sustainable carbon budgets[c]
World[d]	4.5	29	2
Australia	16.2	104	7
Canada	20.0	129	9
France	6.0	39	3
Germany	9.8	63	4
Italy	7.8	50	3
Japan	9.9	63	4
Netherlands	8.7	56	4
United Kingdom	9.8	63	4
United States	20.6	132	9

Source: UNDP, Human Development Report 2007, calculations based on Indicator Table 24.

a. As measured in sustainable carbon budgets.
b. Refers to global emissions if every country in the world emitted at the same per capita level as the specified country.
c. Based on a sustainable emissions pathway of 14.5 Gt CO_2 per year.
d. Current global carbon footprint.

6.12.5 Concentrations of Particulate Matter and Sulfur Dioxide

In addition to the global environment, developing countries also have to deal with local environmental challenges. Particularly in urban areas, air pollution can be the cause of severe respiratory diseases, and children are most at risk. Water pollution and the availability of water is another daunting challenge.

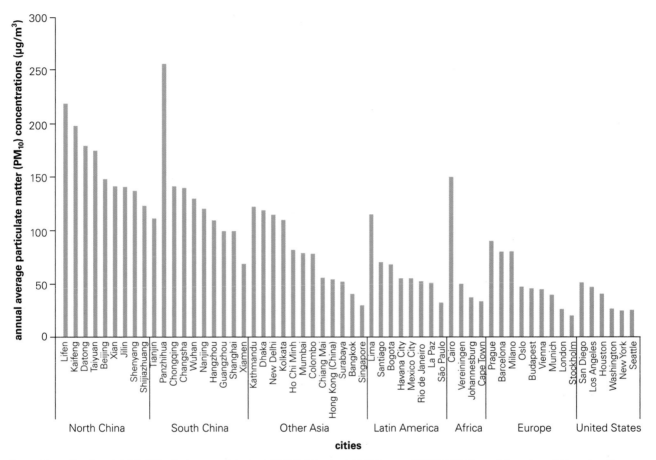

Source: Liang, Congjie, ed. 2005. *China Environmental Yearbook 2005.* Brill Academic Publishers; and WHO 2005. Copy of figure is available at: http://siteresources.worldbank.org/INTEAPREGTOPENVIRONMENT/Resources/China_Cost_of_Pollution.pdf, p. xviii.

*The notation PM10 is used to describe airborne particles of 10 micrometers or less.

Glossary

Agglomeration: The geographical clustering of economic activity.

Agglomeration Externalities: The benefits of clustering—such as the ready availability of a pool of skilled workers—for which firms do not pay.

Budget deficit: What results when a government spends more than it can raise in revenues.

Capital Account: Countries record their economic transactions with other nations in a national ledger called the balance of payments. The capital account is the part of this ledger where they record cross-border trade in assets—such as bonds or shares. It thus tracks the flow of capital into and out of the country.

Catch-Up: The process by which less developed economies tend to grow at faster rates than industrialized economies because they can replicate modern economies' production methods, institutions, and technologies rather than developing them from scratch.

Clean Development Mechanism: An arrangement under the Kyoto Protocol (which came into force in 2005) that allows industrialized countries to invest in reducing emissions in developing countries as an alternative to reducing them in their own countries.

Creative Destruction: A phrase popularized by the economist Joseph Schumpeter. In his vision of capitalism, entrepreneurs enter markets with new products and production techniques that create value even as they destroy the worth of existing companies.

Current Account: Like the capital account (see above), the current account is part of a country's balance of payments, recording its transactions with the rest of the world. The current account records earnings from exports; expenditures on imports; unilateral transfers, such as migrant remittances; and the net income the country earns from its net holdings of foreign assets. Thus, while the purchase of a foreign bond would be recorded in the capital account, the interest received on that bond would be recorded in the current account.

Current-Account Deficit: A country runs a current-account deficit when its current receipts from the rest of the world fall short of its current payments to it. In other words it receives less income from its exports of foreign assets than it must pay to other countries to import their goods, or to service its foreign debt. To run a current-account deficit, a country must borrow from the rest of the world, or must sell assets.

Economic Diversification: Creating a variety of new economic activities and industries—implying that the share of traditional sectors, typically agriculture, goes down.

Foreign Direct Investment: Capital inflows from outside the country that create or add to company assets, such as plant and equipment. An important feature of these flows is that they are not readily reversible, unlike some financial flows.

Gini Coefficient: A measure of income inequality, which ranges from zero (everyone has the same income) to one (one person receives all the income). Most countries for which there are estimates have Gini coefficients between 0.25 (Sweden in 2000) and 0.59 (Brazil in 2001).

Global Imbalances: The current worldwide pattern of saving and spending, which is marked by excess saving in Asia and the Middle East and excess spending in America. These patterns result in large current-account surpluses in Asia and the Middle East and a big current-account deficit in America.

Import Substitution: A government policy that attempts to replace imports with domestically produced goods.

Industrial Policies: Any government regulation or spending that aims to promote a particular industry or firm. In developing countries, industrial policies are often intended to encourage export diversification whereas in industrialized countries they are intended to push forward the technological frontier.

Inflation Targeting: An approach to central banking in which a target rate of inflation is announced, and the central bank then attempts to steer actual inflation toward the target using interest rates and other tools.

Labor surplus: Where the labor provided is in excess of the labor necessary to carry out an activity.

Market Incentives: The incentive to increase profitable activities and decrease unprofitable ones, based on the demand for goods and services and the cost of providing them.

Mitigation: Reduction in the severity of adverse conditions. In the context of global warming, mitigation refers to cuts in the emission of greenhouse gases, or to other, offsetting measures that reduce the amount of warming for a given concentration of greenhouse gases.

Resource Mobility: The ease with which labor and capital move from industry to industry, or region to region.

Resource Rents: The surplus value of natural resources, such as oil, after all costs have been accounted for.

Static Analysis: Investigating the properties of an economy or market "at rest," when market forces are in a settled equilibrium. The analysis usually proceeds by changing one or more variables, while assuming that underlying parameters remain the same and ignoring the path taken from the initial situation to the amended one. For example, a static analysis might compare the production costs of a small firm to those of a larger firm, assuming that tastes and technology remained the same.

Structural Diversification: A major change in a country's economy that involves extending economic activities into different fields. This may involve the reform or creation of new economic institutions.

Structural Transformation: A fundamental shift in a country's methods of economic organization, such as the reallocation of labor, physical, and human capital among agriculture, manufacturing, and services industries. This involves the addition of activities and the removal of other activities that are no longer economically viable or profitable.

Acknowledgments

Experts and academics have helped the Commission become aware of the state of the art in a variety of areas, including issues that serious academic research has not yet settled, and in which a range of views exists. They have contributed with papers they wrote, presentations they made, and inputs they offered to the discussions both within and outside the workshops during the last two years. Their contributions have been critical to our work. Although any expression of acknowledgment will fail to fully capture the importance of their role, I would still like to thank each of them, and also to say how much I and my fellow Commissioners appreciated their contributions and enjoyed our interactions. I would also like to thank all those that helped the workshops become a reality, and all others who, in various capacities, helped this project come to a successful conclusion.

Michael Spence
June 2008

Secretariat

Darlington, Muriel
Hesse, Heiko
Manevskaya, Diana
Nowak, Dorota
Singh, Pavneet
Ticha, Ivana
Yenko, Marie
Zagha, Roberto

Communications Team

Brahmam, Maya, World Bank
Cullen, Tim, Consultant
Fisher, Paul, Consultant
Viveros, Alejandra, World Bank

Editor

Cox, Simon, The Economist

Statistical Appendix

Jiang, Teng, World Bank

Publications

Bergeron, Denise, World Bank
Chen, Shaohua, World Bank
Gnanasundram, Pushpa, World Bank
Gökdemir, Aziz, World Bank
Lammers, Nancy, World Bank
Lanjouw, Peter, World Bank
McGroarty, Stephen, World Bank
Pombo, Santiago, World Bank
Sangraula, Prem, World Bank

Web Site and Blog

Afif, Zeina, World Bank
Alexis, Cindy, World Bank
Del Rosario, Jorge F., World Bank
Kuehl, Liz, FreeRange Studios
M'chich, Karim, World Bank
Mishra, Swati Priyadarshini, World Bank
Ozimek, Ryan, PICNet
Wielezynski, Pierre Guillaume, World Bank

Workshop Participants and Paper Authors

Abdel-Rahman, Hesham, University of New Orleans
Ahluwalia, Isher, Board of Governors of the Indian Council for Research on International Economic Relations (ICRIER)
Alam, Asad, World Bank
Albrecht, James, Georgetown University
Alleyne, George, Pan American Health Organization
Alm, James, Georgia State University
Altenburg, Tilman, German Development Institute
Angel, Solly, New York University
Aninat, Cristóbal, Ministry of External Affairs, Chile
Anos Casero, Paloma, World Bank
Aoki, Masahiko, Stanford University
Asabere, Paul, Temple University
Atlas, Scott, Stanford University
Backeus, Karl, Ministry of Foreign Affairs of Sweden
Bain, Laurel, Eastern Caribbean Central Bank, St. Kitts and Nevis
Banerji, Arup, World Bank
Barr, Nicholas, London School of Economics
Behrman, Jere, University of Pennsylvania
Benabou, Roland, Princeton University
Bertaud, Alain, Consultant

Bhattacharya, Amar, G-24 Secretariat

Bhorat, Haroon, University of Cape Town (South Africa)

Birdsall, Nancy, Center for Global Development

Bleakley, Hoyt, University of Chicago

Bloom, David, Harvard University

Bloom, Nick, Stanford University

Blyde, Juan, Inter-American Development Bank

Bosworth, Barry, The Brookings Institution

Bourguignon, François, Paris School of Economics

Bowles, Samuel, Santa Fe Institute and University of Siena

Braga, Carlos, World Bank

Brueckner, Jan, University of California at Irvine

Bruggenkamp, Ammarens, Embassy of the Netherlands in the United States

Calderon, Cesar, World Bank

Cardoso, Fernando Henrique, former President of Brazil

Caselli, Francesco, London School of Economics

Chawla, Mukesh, World Bank

Chiquier, Loic, World Bank

Cho, Man, The Korea Development Institute (KDI) School

Cichello, Paul, World Bank

Cooper, Richard, Harvard University

Cottarelli, Carlo, International Monetary Fund

Cunha, Flavio, University of Pennsylvania

Dadush, Uri, World Bank

De Mello, Luiz, OECD

Deichmann, Uwe, World Bank

Dhar, Sanjay, World Bank

Dobronogov, Anton, World Bank

Eldhagen, Erik, World Bank

Ellis, Randall, Boston University

Engel, Eduardo, Yale University

Fares, Jean, World Bank

Fatás, Antonio, Professor, INSEAD

Fernandes-Arias, Eduardo, Inter-American Development Bank

Ferreira, Francisco, World Bank

Fields, Gary, Cornell University

Filmer, Deon, World Bank

Fischer, Ronald, University of Chile

Fisman, Raymond, Columbia University

Fleischmann, Alan, ImagiNations

Fortson, Jane, University of Chicago

Fox, Louise, World Bank

Freeman, Richard, National Bureau of Economic Research
Freire, Maria Emilia, World Bank
Fuhr, Harald, University of Potsdam
Geelen, M.W.M.S., Ministry of Foreign Affairs, The Netherlands
Gelb, Alan, World Bank
Gertler, Paul, University of California, Berkeley
Giavazzi, Francesco, Bocconi University (Italy) and Massachusetts
    Institute of Technology
Giles, John, World Bank
Gordon, Roger, University of California, San Diego
Gottret, Pablo, World Bank
Green, Richard, George Washington University
Grigonyte, Dalia, The European Commission
Gutierrez, Catalina, World Bank
Gwinner, William, World Bank
Haacker, Markus, International Monetary Fund
Hagan, Harry, Department for International Development (DFID),
    United Kingdom
Haltiwanger, John, University of Maryland
Hammer, Jeffrey, Princeton University
Hannah, Lawrence, World Bank
Hanson, Gordon, University of California, San Diego
Hanushek, Eric, The Hoover Institution, Stanford University
Harrison, Ann, University of California-Berkeley
Hartler, Christina, SIDA
Healey, Paul, Department for International Development (DFID),
    United Kingdom
Hegedüs, József, Metropolitan Research Institute, Budapest (Hungary)
Henderson, Vernon, Brown University
Holzmann, Robert, World Bank
Hwang, Min, George Washington University
Ikhsan, Mohamad, Coordinating Ministry for Economic Affairs
    of Indonesia
Jack, William, Georgetown University
Jaramillo, Carlos Felipe, World Bank
Johnson, Simon, International Monetary Fund
Jones, Ben, Northwestern University
Joshi, Manosh, Embassy of India, Washington, DC
Jousten, Alain, International Monetary Fund
King, Elizabeth, World Bank
Kingsmill, William, Department for International Development (DFID),
    United Kingdom
Klasen, Stephan, University of Goettingen

Kumar, Manmohan Singh, Visiting Professor, Georgetown University
Kumar, Rajiv, Indian Council of International Economic Relations
Laszek, Jacek, Central Bank of Poland
Leamer, Edward, University of California-Los Angeles
Lederman, Daniel, World Bank
Lee, Chung Min, National University of Singapore
Levy, Santiago, Inter-American Development Bank
Lewis, Maureen, World Bank
Linn, Johannes, The Brookings Institution
Logan, John, Brown University
Lombardi, Domenico, The Oxford Institute for Economic Policy
    and The Brookings Institution
Lucas, Robert, University of Chicago
Lundstrom, Susanna, World Bank
MacCallum, Lisa, The Nike Foundation
Mahajan, Sandeep, World Bank
Mahbub Al-Matin, Kazi, World Bank
Mahovsky, Madeleine, The European Commission
Malpezzi, Steve, University of Wisconsin-Madison
May, Ernesto, World Bank
Meadows, Graham, European Research Institute, University of Sussex
Mendelsohn, Robert, Yale University
Merchant, Ann, World Bank
Mohanty, P. K., Ministry of Urban Development and Poverty Alleviation,
    Government of India
Moreno-Dodson, Blanca, World Bank
Morrison, Andrew, World Bank
Mowery, David, University of California-Berkeley
Mulas, Alberto, SHF, Mexico City
Mustafaoglu, Zafer, World Bank
Nabli, Mustapha, World Bank
Naim, Moises, Foreign Policy Magazine
Nankani, Gobind, Global Development Network
Nehru, Vikram, World Bank
Nero, Jennifer, Eastern Caribbean Central Bank (St. Kitts and Nevis)
Nichols, Garth, Eastern Caribbean Central Bank (St. Kitts and Nevis)
Nordhaus, William, Yale University
Obstfeld, Maurice, University of California Berkeley
Olsen, Edgar, University of Virginia
Opper, Barbara, U.S. Treasury Office of Technical Assistance
Ozden, Caglar, World Bank
Ozer, Ceren, World Bank
Pack, Howard, University of Pennsylvania

Palmade, Vincent, International Finance Corporation
Patrinos, Harry, World Bank
Perotti, Roberto, University of Bocconi (Italy)
Perry, Guillermo, World Bank
Peterson, George, The Urban Institute
Pinto, Brian, World Bank
Pritchett, Lant, Center for Global Development
Rajan, Raghuram, University of Chicago
Ramachandran, S., World Bank
Ramos, Maria, Transnet, Ltd. (South Africa)
Renaud, Bertaud, World Bank
Rivlin, Alice, The Brookings Institution
Rodriguez-Clare, Andres, Penn State University
Rodrik, Dani, Harvard University
Rosenzweig, Mark, Yale University
Rossi-Hansberg, Esteban, Princeton University
Sanchez Puerta, Maria Laura, World Bank
Sasin, Marcin, World Bank
Schady, Norbert, World Bank
Segal, Susan, Americas Society and Council of the Americas
Sheppard, Stephen, Williams College
Shiller, Robert, Yale University
Simler, Kenneth, World Bank
Singh, Smita, Flora and William Hewlett Foundation
Sjoblom, Mirja, World Bank
Sridhar, Shri S., National Housing Bank, Government of India
Srinivasan, T. N., Yale University
Stehn, Sven Jari, International Monetary Fund
Stephens, Mark, The University of York (United Kingdom)
Suarez, Reuben, Pan-American Health Organization
Svejnar, Jan, University of Michigan
Tanzi, Vito, International Monetary Fund
Ter-Minassian, Teresa, International Monetary Fund
Thalwitz, Margret, World Bank
Toruan, Henry, Coordinating Ministry for Economic Affairs of Indonesia
Tybout, James, Pennsylvania State University
Udry, Christopher, Yale University
Van den Noord, Paul, The European Commission
Van Gelder, Linda, World Bank
Van Order, Robert, University of Michigan
Vashakmadze, Ekaterine, World Bank
Villani, Kevin, San Diego State University
Viveros, Alejandra, World Bank

Vodopivec, Milan, World Bank
Vyborny, Kate, Center for Global Development
Wacziarg, Romain, Stanford University
Wallace, William, World Bank
Warner, Andrew, Millennium Challenge Corporation
Watkins, Alfred, World Bank
Weil, David, Brown University
Whitehead, Christine, London School of Economics
Wong, Grace, University of Pennsylvania
Woodruff, Chris, University of California, San Diego
Wu, Weiping, Virginia Commonwealth University
Wyplosz, Charles, Graduate School of International and Development
    Studies, Geneva (Switzerland)
Yezer, Anthony, George Washington University
Yusuf, Shahid, World Bank

Authors of Papers and Case Studies

Acemoglu, Daron, Massachusetts Institute of Technology
Aghion, Philippe, Harvard University
Ahmed, Sadiq, World Bank
Arnott, Richard, University of California-Riverside
Attanasio, Orazio, University College London
Banerjee, Abhijit, Massachusetts Institute of Technology
Bernardo, Romeo, Lazaro, Bernardo Tiu, and Associates, Inc.
Bhattasali, Deepak, World Bank
Bloom, David, Harvard University
Brady, David, Stanford University
Brenton, Paul, World Bank
Canning, David, Harvard University
Cárdenas, Mauricio, Fedesarollo (Colombia)
Cardoso, Fernando-Henrique, former President of Brazil
Cline, William, Peterson Institute for International Economics and the
    Center for Global Development
Collier, Paul, University of Oxford
Das, Jishnu, World Bank
Demirguc-Kunt, Asli, World Bank
Dickens, William, University of Maryland
Duranton, Gilles, University of Toronto
Durlauf, Steven, University of Wisconsin-Madison
Eichengreen, Barry, University of California, Berkeley
El Beblawi, Hazem, Arab Monetary Fund
El-Erian, Mohamed, PIMCO
Eng, Alvin, Monetary Authority of Singapore

Estache, Antonio, Université Libre de Bruxelles (Belgium)

Fatas, Antonio, INSEAD

Fay, Marianne, World Bank

Ffrench-Davis, Ricardo, Economic Commission for Latin America and the Caribbean (ECLAC) and University of Chile

Frankel, Jeffrey, Harvard University

Gomez-Ibanez, Jose, Harvard University

Graeff, Eduardo, São Paulo State Government Representation Office in Brasília

Hakimian, Hassan, Cass Business School (United Kingdom)

Hesse, Heiko, International Monetary Fund

Hoekman, Bernard, World Bank

Hofman, Bert, World Bank

Iyoha, Milton, Igbinedion University (Nigeria)

Izvorski, Ivailo, World Bank

Jack, William, Georgetown University

Jaffee, Dwight, University of California-Berkeley

Jakubiak, Malgorzata, Center for Social and Economic Research (CASE), (Poland)

Kanbur, Ravi, Cornell University

Kigabo, Thomas, National Bank of Rwanda and National University of Rwanda

Kim, Sukkoo, Washington University in St. Louis

Kolesar, Peter, Center for Social and Economic Research (CASE), (Poland)

Kremer, Michael, Harvard University

Kurekova, Lucia, Central European University (Hungary)

Lehoucq, Fabrice E., University of North Carolina-Greensboro

Levine, Ross, Brown University

Light, Miles, University of Colorado

Loewald, Christopher, Ministry of Finance (South Africa)

Lumiste, Rünno, Tallinn University of Technology (Estonia)

Mahajan, Sandeep, World Bank

Mahmud, Wahiduddin, University of Dhaka (Bangladesh)

Maipose, Gervase, University of Botswana

Mattoo, Aaditya, World Bank

Meghir, Costas, University College London

Mkapa, Benjamin William, former President of Tanzania

Montiel, Peter, Williams College

Ndiaye, Mansour, Proximis International, Dakar

Newfarmer, Richard, World Bank

Page, John, St. Anthony's College, Oxford and World Bank

Pefferly, Robert, Estonian Business School (Estonia)

Purju, Alari, Tallinn University of Technology (Estonia)
Quigley, John, University of California-Berkeley
Rama, Martin, World Bank
Robinson, Edward, Monetary Authority of Singapore
Robinson, James, Harvard University
Rodrik, Dani, Harvard University
Rozo, Sandra, Fedesarollo (Colombia)
Schmidt-Hebbel, Klaus, Central Bank of Chile
Stavrakeva, Vania, The Brookings Institution
Tan, Yin Ying, Monetary Authority of Singapore
Tang, Christine, Lazaro, Bernardo Tiu, and Associates, Inc.
Taymaz, Erol, Middle East Technical University (Turkey)
Varshney, Ashutosh, University of Michigan
Venables, Anthony, Department for International Development (DFID)
    and University of Oxford (United Kingdom)
Vishwanath, Tara, World Bank
Walkenhorst, Peter, World Bank
Werneck, Rogério, Catholic University of Rio de Janeiro (PUC-Rio)
Wheeler, David, Center for Global Development
Williamson, John, Peterson Institute for International Economics
Wu, Tingliang, Development Research Center of the State Council
    (China)
Wyplosz, Charles, The Graduate Institute, Geneva (Switzerland)
Yilmaz, Kamil, Koç University, Turkey
Yusof, Zainal, National Implementation Task Force (Malaysia)

Workshop Organizers

Annez, Patricia, World Bank
Buckley, Robert, The Rockefeller Foundation
Carneiro, Pedro, University College London
Kharas, Homi, Wolfensohn Center for Development, The Brookings
    Institution
Lewis, Maureen, World Bank
Maloney, William, World Bank
Nowak, Dorota, World Bank
Paci, Pierella, World Bank
Peregoy, Joseph, B&B Reporters
Salzman, Randy, B&B Reporters
Serven, Luis, World Bank
Wheeler, Haynie, Center for the Study of Globalization,
    Yale University

Working Group

Carneiro, Pedro, University College London

Kharas, Homi, Wolfensohn Center for Development, The Brookings Institution

Leipziger, Danny, World Bank

Lim, Edwin, China Economic Research and Advisory Programme

Romer, Paul, Stanford University and Hoover Institution

Solow, Robert, Nobel Laureate in Economics and Professor Emeritus, Massachussetts Institute of Technology

Zagha, Roberto, Growth Commission Secretariat and World Bank